STALIN

Stalin must command our unconditional respect. In his own way he is a hell of a fellow. Stalin is half beast, half giant.
—ADOLF HITLER, 1942

X

STALIN

ALBERT MARRIN

Viking Kestrel

PHOTOGRAPH CREDITS
Hulton Picture Library: page 135
The Library of Congress, Washington, D.C.: page 70
The National Archives, Washington, D.C.: pages 48, 72, 111, 123, 156,
186, 197, and 214
The New York Public Library: page 25

Grateful acknowledgment is made for permission to reprint an excerpt from *One Day
in the Life of Ivan Denisovich* by Alexander I. Solzhenitsyn, translated by
Ralph Parker. English translation copyright © 1963 by E. P. Dutton, New York, and
Victor Gollancz Ltd., London. Reprinted by permission of E. P. Dutton, a division of
NAL Penguin Inc., and Victor Gollancz Ltd.

VIKING KESTREL
Published by the Penguin Group
Viking Penguin Inc., 40 West 23rd Street, New York, New York 10010, U.S.A.
Penguin Books Ltd, 27 Wrights Lane, London W8 5TZ, England
Penguin Books Australia Ltd, Ringwood, Victoria, Australia
Penguin Books Canada Ltd, 2801 John Street, Markham, Ontario, Canada L3R 1B4
Penguin Books (N.Z.) Ltd, 182–190 Wairau Road, Auckland 10, New Zealand

Penguin Books Ltd, Registered Offices: Harmondsworth, Middlesex, England

First published in 1988 by Viking Penguin Inc.
Published simultaneously in Canada

1 3 5 7 9 10 8 6 4 2

Copyright © Albert Marrin, 1988
All rights reserved

Library of Congress Cataloging in Publication Data
Marrin, Albert.   Stalin / by Albert Marrin.   p. cm.
Bibliography: p.   Includes index.
Summary: An account of the life of the man who shaped the Soviet
Union, from pre-revolutionary Russia to its evolution as a
superpower and the descent of the "Iron Curtain."
ISBN 0-670-82102-0
1. Stalin, Joseph, 1879–1953—Juvenile literature.   2. Soviet
Union—History—1925–1953—Juvenile literature.   3. Heads of state—
Soviet Union—Biography—Juvenile literature.   [1. Stalin, Joseph,
1879–1953.   2. Heads of state.]   I. Title.
DK268.S8M33   1988   [92]—dc19   88-17345   CIP

Printed in the United States of America by Arcata Graphics, Fairfield, Pennsylvania
Set in Electra

To the Memory of the Innocents

Contents

STALIN

PROLOGUE:
LENIN'S TOMB

RED SQUARE, MOSCOW, RUSSIA, THURSDAY, NOVEMBER 7, 1929.
A cold Moscow morning, with high gray clouds drifting above
damp, glistening cobblestones.

Since before dawn marchers had been assembling near the
vast square outside the Russian capital's ancient fortress, or
Kremlin, a city within a city of palaces, churches, and government buildings. Across from the Kremlin wall stood The
Place of the Head, the execution block to which the rulers of
old Russia had sent countless victims. To the right stood St.
Basil's Cathedral, with its golden, onion-shaped domes, now
an antireligious museum. But the focus of attention was directly in front of the Kremlin wall: a reviewing stand atop a
low building of polished red granite.

The building housed the mummified body of V. I. Lenin.
His open coffin was bathed in red light and the mummy lay
swathed in red velvet, only its face left visible for the hundreds
of thousands who paid their respects every year. Today was a
special day, the twelfth anniversary of the revolution Lenin
had led and of the new Russia he'd created, the Union of
Soviet Socialist Republics. But it wasn't Lenin the marchers
had come to honor.

All eyes were fixed on one man in the reviewing stand. He
was not an impressive figure, not the sort of man you'd notice
in a crowd. Simply dressed, he wore a khaki military tunic
and trousers, stuffed into high black leather boots. He was
short with a low forehead, close-cropped black hair and a
drooping mustache. Deep pockmarks covered his face. When

3

he smiled, which was seldom, he flashed gold-plated teeth, though others were blackened by rot. His complexion was sallow, the result of spending nearly all his time indoors in offices. A month shy of his fiftieth birthday, he moved slowly, spoke softly, and seemed always to be in perfect control. For his people, he was the Vozhd—the Leader.

His name was Joseph Stalin, and he was the most important man in the Communist world. Today was his day, for after years of scheming, he'd beaten his opponents. Now he alone ruled the largest country on earth.

The parade began as soon as Stalin took his place. Columns of Red Army men led the way, their boots thundering on the cobblestones, their bayonet-tipped rifles thrust before them, inches from the backs of the ranks in front. Tanks, artillery, and armored cars rumbled after them. After the army had passed, a million Muscovites swarmed into Red Square to the accompaniment of brass bands. Bobbing amid this sea of humanity were larger-than-life portraits of Stalin, Lenin, and other Communist leaders. Red hammer-and-sickle flags and red banners emblazoned with slogans in golden letters were everywhere—as were the dreaded "bluecaps." Thousands of these secret policemen lined both sides of the square, watching every face and gesture.

As the marchers neared the reviewing stand, they chanted "Slava velikomu Stalinu!" No sooner did one group pass than another took up the cry: "Slava velikomu Stalinu!" "Glory to Great Stalin!" But they wouldn't have been so enthusiastic had they known what he had in store for them.

When Stalin was still a boy, a Russian writer described the tragedy of his country: "Unhappy nation, nation of slaves; high and low, all are slaves." Russia has known many oppressors in its long history. Viking war chiefs, Mongol khans, Russian tsars—all had brought the people misery. But even Genghis

Khan, who heaped up mounds of severed heads, or Tsar Ivan the Terrible, who invented horrible tortures, seem mild when compared to "Great Stalin." Stalin dashed the hopes of the Russian people for freedom, fastening upon them a tyranny worse than they'd ever known or imagined.

For a quarter of a century he would rule unopposed, with a fist of iron and a heart of stone, the only free person in a country of 190,000,000. Free from criticism or control, bound by no belief in law or morality, Stalin's power was limitless.

Stalin did whatever he pleased, whenever he pleased, to whomever he pleased. He commanded cities to rise where there'd been only nomads' tents. He decided how people earned their livings and raised their children. His tastes in art and music determined what Russians would see and hear. He uprooted entire nations and resettled them thousands of miles from their homes. People believed what he wanted them to believe—or else.

Stalin knew only two punishments for disobedience: quick death by shooting or slow death by starvation, cold, and overwork. No fewer than twenty million of his people were killed *in peacetime*, while other tens of millions toiled in the *gulag*, his slave labor camps. He may justly be numbered among the two or three worst men who ever lived; surely he was the greatest mass murderer of all time, outdoing even Adolf Hitler, whom he admired and who admired him.

Under Stalin's iron hand, Russia became a superpower. Today, more than a generation after Stalin's death, his influence is still felt in every area of Soviet life. Thus, to understand him enables us to better understand the nation he shaped. And that is good, because only by understanding can we hope to ensure that there will, indeed, be future generations.

THE REBEL

JOSEPH VISSARIONOVICH DJUGASHVILI—THE FUTURE STALIN—
was born December 21, 1879, in the town of Gori on the
southern slopes of the Caucasus Mountains. This is glorious
country. Swift rivers, fed by runoff from snowcapped peaks,
course through fertile valleys. Wheat is plentiful, as well as
grapes, which yield scores of tasty wines. There are also rich
grazing lands, where herds of sheep and goats fatten quickly.

Gori, in the province of Georgia, also has a rich heritage.
Georgia, seized by the Russian Empire in the eighteenth century, is at the crossroads of Europe and Asia. Many peoples—
Greeks, Romans, Persians, Mongols, Turks, Armenians—had
settled there, each leaving its mark on the province's customs
and language. When Soso (Georgian for "Joey") Djugashvili
was born, many still lived as their ancestors had during the
Middle Ages. In some villages men wore coats of chain mail
handed down from the Crusaders. In Gori, bearded men strolled
the streets with silver-handled daggers thrust into their belts.

These weapons weren't for show. Although a cheerful people, enjoying good companionship and good food, Georgians
had fiery tempers. The vendetta, or blood feud, was a tradition.
If a man was hurt or insulted, let alone killed, no one thought
of going to the authorities. It was the duty of every member
of his family to take bloody vengeance upon the guilty party
or his nearest relatives.

Everyone knew the folktale about the chieftain who killed
a rival and then murdered his wife and children. "Don't you
understand?" he said when questioned about the murders.

"Once you have jumped over with your forelegs, jump over with your hindlegs as well. Once you begin killing a [family], kill them all. Leave no future avenger." Soso took the chieftain's advice to heart and followed it throughout his lifetime. The youngster had plenty to feel vengeful about. He was born into a desperately poor family. The Djugashvili house was merely a dingy hut with wooden walls and a brick floor. Outside was an alley with an open sewer running down the middle. The place stank of foul water and unwashed bodies.

Yet such surroundings alone did not make Soso vengeful. Decent people have come from worse circumstances than his. But a child needs a stable home and, unfortunately, his home was anything but stable. His mother, Ekaterina—Catherine— was a peasant's daughter who'd married at fifteen and lost her first three children at birth. When her fourth survived, she thought him such a blessing that she named him after Saint Joseph. His father, Vissarion, however, was one of life's losers. Nothing he did turned out well. A self-employed shoemaker, he was a boor and a bully with a violent temper. When he got drunk, anything, or nothing, might send his fists flying.

Vissarion often grabbed little Soso with one hand and beat him with the other, stopping only when he grew tired. Townspeople shook their heads when they saw Soso in the streets with black eyes, his body a mass of purple bruises. Vissarion also beat his wife in front of the boy. Once Soso tried to defend her by throwing a knife at his father. He missed, the brute bellowed like an angry bull and charged. Soso ran away and hid with neighbors until the storm passed.

Our best picture of young Soso comes from Joseph Iremashvili, one of the neighborhood boys who often visited Soso's home and became his best friend. Though Stalin would later kill nearly everyone who'd known him as a child, he spared Iremashvili's life. Instead, he expelled Iremashvili from

the Soviet Union in the 1920s. He lived in Germany where
he wrote a book, *Stalin and the Tragedy of Georgia*.

Iremashvili described a child who was small for his age and
who'd never be taller than five feet four. He had dark hair and
brown eyes that seemed to look into people, reading their
innermost thoughts. His face was deeply pitted from a smallpox
attack that nearly killed him. Blood poisoning developed from
a bruise on his left arm, probably caused by Vissarion's fist;
the arm became three inches shorter than his right, remaining
lame and useless for the rest of his life.

What most impressed Iremashvili was the way the beatings
shaped the youngster's character. "I never saw him crying,"
he recalled. "Those undeserved and fearful beatings made the
boy as . . . heartless as his father." They taught him to hate.
At first he hated his father, but in time his hatred embraced
all of humanity. They also made him hard. He, too, wore
armor, an inner armor of self-defenses stronger than any chain
mail. It shielded him from human feeling, making him unable
to feel others' pain or sympathize with their suffering.

When Soso was five, his father went to work in a shoe factory
in another town. Although he visited Gori from time to time,
he never again lived with his family. Always restless, he became
a tramp and died around 1890 in a tavern brawl. His death
must have come as a relief to his son. Iremashvili recalled:
"In the man he was supposed to call father he lost nothing."

Meantime, Ekaterina had to support herself and her child.
It wasn't easy. Usually she worked in rich people's homes,
scrubbing floors, doing laundry, and running errands. Sometimes she took work home, sitting up nights sewing other
people's underwear by the light of a kerosene lamp. If there
wasn't any work, she became desperate. She'd wander about
town, her hair wild, crying, praying, and muttering to herself.
Yet she always managed to keep her Soso clean and neat, even

if he sometimes went to bed hungry. She was the only person he loved.

A quiet, pious woman, Ekaterina's only pleasure was attending the local Russian Orthodox church. The church, with its services and music, was an island of beauty and peace in her harsh world. Her only ambition was for her Soso to become a priest and to bless her with his own hands. For his part, he enjoyed going to church. He had a pleasant voice and became a choirboy, singing hymns and taking part in religious processions.

When Soso turned nine, she sent him to the local church school. On his first day he found that he stood out like an ugly duckling. His schoolmates, mostly the sons of prosperous craftsmen and shopkeepers, always seemed happier than he. This deepened his sense of inferiority and made him bitter. He was always sarcastic, always eager to laugh at others' expense. Their misfortunes were deserved, their joys mere silliness, he'd sneer. To Soso friendship meant following his lead and agreeing with everything he said. Despite his handicap, he was a wiry youngster with a strong right arm. Anyone who disagreed with him—and was weaker—got a fist in the face. In short, he was your typical school bully.

Still, Soso was a good pupil. Intelligent and eager to learn, he enjoyed reading and soon went through every book in the school library. His lessons were always ready in time and well prepared. Nothing was allowed to get in the way of his schoolwork. Even when he was running a high fever, he insisted on studying to keep up his grades. His efforts paid off, and his teachers decided that he deserved to continue his education. After passing the entrance examination, he received a scholarship to the theological seminary in Tiflis, the capital of Georgia. His mother's prayers were being answered. Her son was on his way to becoming a priest—or so she thought.

*Stalin (top row, center) and classmates at the
Gori Ecclesiastical Scollo around 1888.*

Soso hated the seminary from the moment its gates closed behind him. He always remembered it as a prison, complete with barred windows, rather than as a school. Except for two free hours in the afternoon, the students' day was a steady grind of work and prayer, and prayer hurt. They'd stand for hours on one spot, unable to shift their weight, so that their legs swelled and their backs ached. There were hundreds of rules, few of which seemed just or sensible. Yet the least infraction brought time in a stone dungeon called the Dark Room. The black-robed monks, fearing the influence of "dangerous books," spied on the students constantly. Often the students would return from meals to find that their rooms had been searched.

The students resented such treatment and, as good Georgians, doubly resented the Russian monks, who represented the conquering tsars and regarded Georgians as inferiors. The Georgian language sounded, to Russians, like the speech of wild men. A few years before Soso's arrival, a student beat the principal for making nasty remarks about Georgia; another teenager later shot him to death. Students went on strike several times to demand an end to the harsh discipline and to social injustice. Soso also bridled under this discipline. He joined a student group that met secretly to read and discuss the "dangerous books" and debate on the injustices beyond the seminary. It was in this group that Soso made the discovery that would be a turning point in his life. To understand how he arrived at this, we must first understand something of the Russian Empire in which he grew up.

Old Russia consisted of many nationalities ruled by an emperor known as the Tsar of All the Russias. The largest nationality was the Great Russians, followed by the Ukrainians and White Russians. Smaller nationalities included the Georgians and Volga Germans, Moldavians, Armenians, and Crimean Tartars. These peoples belonged to almost all the great world religions and spoke some two hundred different languages.

Russia, the heart of the empire, had grown up through the Middle Ages from a log-hut village beside the Moscow River. Over the centuries, the tsars expanded their domain in every direction. Their armies, often spearheaded by Cossacks, fierce warriors born to the saddle, were so successful that they came to rule the largest empire in history. Their empire stretched unbroken from the Bering Strait to the Austrian border, from Sweden to Persia, spanning eleven time zones and covering one-sixth of the earth's land mass.

When Soso Djugashvili was born, this vast empire was known as "the prison of the peoples." Its tsar was an autocrat, one who ruled by himself and had unlimited authority. He alone appointed government officials and made the laws. There were no elections, no parliaments, no courts to check the actions of one responsible to God alone. "Everything," said the proverb, "is under the power of God and the tsar."

The tsar's subjects knew nothing of the civil liberties that other nations took for granted. Political parties were forbidden, existing only in secret. Nothing could be printed if it challenged the tsar's authority; newspapers were shut down for mentioning injustices or questioning government actions.

Over eighty percent of Russia's citizens were *mujiks*, peasant farmers scattered among thousands of tiny villages. Once they had been serfs, unfree workers who could be bought, sold, and beaten by their masters, the nobility who helped the tsar rule. Although freed in 1861, two years before Abraham Lincoln freed America's slaves, they were still as miserable as ever.

Desperately poor, eking out a living on tiny parcels of land, nineteen out of every twenty peasants died before the age of sixty. The typical peasant family lived in a thatch-roofed hut with an earthen floor and windows, not of glass, but of dried .

cow bladders that hardly let in any light. Instead of beds, most peasants slept on rough wooden benches, which they also used for sitting and eating. Bedding was simply ticking stuffed with straw and swarming with bedbugs. Since there was no plumbing, water had to be drawn from a well, which was often polluted. Sanitation facilities were nonexistent; indeed, human and animal filth was kept at home in buckets for fertilizer. Mostly illiterate and highly superstitious, peasants believed evil spirits brought disease. And disease raged year-round: influenza in winter, malaria in spring, cholera in summer, diphtheria in fall, tuberculosis and smallpox a constant threat.

Yet hunger was the mujik's worst problem, as seen in this traditional poem:

> A Tsar rules the world,
> A Tsar without mercy,
> And Hunger is his name.

The mujik's basic food was a watery cabbage soup eaten with black bread, plus small amounts of milk, butter, and vegetables; if a family was really lucky, it might see a few ounces of meat each week. But since fields were small and crops had to be sold to pay taxes, most families spent their lives hungry. Underfed mothers couldn't feed their babies. Unable to produce milk, they'd chew a crust of bread into a mush, wrap it in a piece of rag, and give it to their babies to suck. As a result, two out of three peasant babies died before their first birthday. Small wonder that mujiks dreamed of having more land to farm. Land meant full stomachs, health, and happiness. It meant being a person. There'd come a time when they'd kill for land.

About the time of Soso's birth, industries began to spring up in cities such as Moscow, St. Petersburg, and Kiev. Europe's richest oil field was opened at Baku, a short railway journey from Gori. By the time Soso entered the seminary, Russia's production of textiles, chemicals, and machinery was steadily increasing. Since there was plenty of work in the new factories, millions of peasants left the land in the hope of finding a better life. What they found was more misery.

Russian workers experienced all the hardships endured by European and American workers in the early stages of their industrial revolutions. Long hours at low wages were normal. The workday in many factories began at four in the morning and lasted until ten at night, eighteen hours a day, seven days a week, month after month without letup. "I did not live, but only worked, worked, and worked," metalworker Ivan Babushkin recalled. "I worked morning, noon, and night, and sometimes did not leave the factory for two days at a stretch."

Factories were built for profit, not safety. Equipment was unprotected, so that a person could easily lose an arm or leg to the whirling wheels. Poisonous chemicals were another threat. The air in match factories, for example, was filled with sulphur, which turned workers' skin yellow and corroded their lungs, making them cough up gobs of blood until they died. No laws held employers responsible for workers crippled or killed in their factories. There were, however, strict laws against forming unions and striking. Strikes were broken up by Cossacks swinging leather whips.

Although factory workers earned more than peasants, their wages didn't go very far. When Soso was a boy, a Russian earned half of what someone doing the same job earned in England or the United States. He brought home between fifteen and forty-five *cents* a day, this when boots cost a year's wages. Most workers never owned a new piece of clothing, but wore whatever they could get from the rag sellers. Trousers, shirts, and coats were patched, then the patches were patched, until the garment resembled a crazy quilt.

Workers never made enough to own their own homes. Unmarried men lived in company-owned barracks that stank to high heaven and swarmed with vermin, each man sleeping on a wooden platform two feet wide by six feet long. Married workers shared a single room. In Moscow two families often lived in a room eight feet by fourteen feet, crowded so tightly that children had to sleep in a trunk or a bureau drawer.

Since men found it impossible to support families on their wages, wives and children had to work. Pregnant women worked even when labor pains began for fear of being fired for leaving work to give birth. It was not uncommon for a woman to have her baby on the factory floor, its wailing drowned by the clatter and clang of the machines. A day or two later, she'd be back at her machine with her infant in a basket next to her; there were no factory nurseries, so mothers had to keep their children with them in order to nurse.

A system that forced people to live under such conditions was bound to be challenged. As early as the 1860s, societies with names such as People's Freedom and Land and Liberty worked to overthrow tsarism. "Pick up your axes!" cried a rebel named Zaichnevsky. "Attack the imperial party without mercy. . . . Kill them in the public squares . . . kill them in their homes, kill them in the narrow city alleys, kill them on the wide metropolitan streets, kill them in the villages and hamlets."

These were no idle threats. Meeting in small, secret groups, workers and students planned their attacks. Policemen were stabbed in the street, their assassins escaping into the crowds. Government officials were shot and bombs tossed into cafés crowded with army officers. In March 1881, when Soso Djugashvili was not yet two, Russia was startled by the most daring attack of all. As Tsar Alexander II rode in his sleigh near the Winter Palace in St. Petersburg, a youth threw a bomb,

wounding one of his Cossack escorts. When Alexander stepped
from the sleigh to comfort the man, another youth threw a
bomb, blowing away his legs and killing him.

Alexander III, the new tsar, began a massive crackdown.
Within weeks of his father's death, he created the Okhrana—
"the security"—which soon grew into the world's largest secret
police force. The Okhrana became the tsar's eyes and ears. Its
agents penetrated every revolutionary group at home and among
Russian exiles in Western Europe and the United States. These
agents not only supplied information, but acted as *agents
provocateurs*, encouraging suspected rebels to break the law so
they could be arrested. In this way thousands of revolutionaries
were stopped before they could do real harm. They were then
"put on ice"—sent to Siberia.

Siberia is a land of vast open spaces, priceless resources, and
freezing winters where the temperature can fall to − 104 degrees Fahrenheit. Throughout tsarist times, criminals and revolutionaries were sent to Siberia. Those guilty of violent crimes
were sentenced to forced labor. They worked in chains building
roads, lumbering, and mining, encouraged by guards who
wielded the knout, a whip of knotted cords that could cut a
man to pieces. Escapes were rare, since it took a special kind
of person to brave the distances and cold.

Revolutionaries innocent of violent crimes, however, were
sentenced to a term of exile. Siberian exile under the tsars was
mild, compared to what it would be under Stalin. If a prisoner
had permission and money, he could come on his own, unguarded, by way of the Trans-Siberian Railway. When he
arrived at his destination, he reported to the police, who assigned him to a village. Except for the fact that he couldn't
leave his assigned area, he was free. He might rent a house,
take a job, hunt with a rifle, study, and get married; exiles
were often joined by their families.

Still, exile was no holiday. A youngster named Leon Trotsky, who we'll meet again later, recalled his Siberian home:

> Life was dark and repressed, utterly remote from the rest of the world. At night, the cockroaches filled the house with their rustlings as they crawled over table and bed, and even over our faces. From time to time we had to move out of the hut for a day or so and keep the door wide open, at a temperature of 35 degrees [Fahrenheit] below zero. In the summer our lives were made miserable by midges. They even bit to death a cow which had lost its way in the woods. The peasants wore nets of tarred horsehair over their heads. In the spring and autumn the village was buried in mud. . . . I was studying Marx, brushing the cockroaches off the page.

Soso was also studying Karl Marx in his secret discussion group in the seminary. Marx's book *Das Kapital—Capital*—was among the group's favorites. Written originally in German and printed in 1867, Russian translations of this work circulated widely among students in the tsar's empire, as did a shorter work Marx wrote in 1848 with his friend Friedrich Engels: *The Communist Manifesto*.

Marx was the leading socialist thinker of his time. Socialism is hard to define, because people who called themselves socialists often didn't agree on what they meant by the term. There are many different brands of socialism. In Germany, for example, they ranged from Social Democracy, which believed in human equality and free elections, to National Socialism, Adolf Hitler's Nazi Party, which hoped to enslave "inferior races" and rule by force.

The one thing they did agree on was that people should not think only of themselves, accumulating riches at the expense of their fellowmen. The solution was "socialism," putting the interests of society ahead of any one individual or group. Most socialists believed in democracy and wanted to bring about change peacefully, through free elections. They wanted the government to own key industries—steel mills, factories, coal mines, electric power plants, railroads, banks—and run them, not for profit, but to meet people's needs. But they also believed that citizens should own their own small businesses and that farmers should have their own land, provided they didn't accumulate large estates worked by poor peasants.

Marx's brand of socialism is called Marxism or "communism," from the Latin *communis*, "held in common" or "belonging to all." Marx believed that businessmen, whom he called "bourgeoisie" and "capitalists," would always oppress the workers, or "proletariat." As the bourgeoisie grew richer, the proletariat would grow more miserable until, in desperation, it revolted. It might be defeated time and again, but would succeed in the end, because, Marx insisted, the "laws of history" were on its side. Victorious at last, it would set up the "dictatorship of the proletariat" to crush all opposition. Under the dictatorship of the proletariat, all factories, farms, and other means of producing goods would belong to society and be used for the benefit of all. People would work at their occupations and receive in turn, not money, but whatever they needed according to the rule: "From each according to his ability; to each according to his need." Once Communists took over in every country, Marx believed nations would disappear and humanity live happily ever after in peace, plenty, and freedom.

Soso Djugashvili's discovery of Marxism changed his life. At last he'd found an outlet for the rage boiling inside him. Iremashvili, also a seminary student, understood what had happened to his friend: "Since all people in authority over others . . . seemed to be like his father, there . . . rose in him a vengeful feeling against all standing above him." Bosses and governors, teachers and priests—he'd make them pay! Pay for his pain! Pay for his shame! He'd destroy the world of the powerful and the prosperous, not out of love for the oppressed, but out of hatred.

The boy who'd sung in church choirs became an atheist, one who denies the existence of God. Religion, he'd tell fellow students, was a sham, a pack of lies invented by the people's oppressors to keep them ignorant and prevent them from fighting for justice. "You know, they are fooling us," he'd say. "There is no God."

Soso began to lead a double life. During the day, he continued his religious studies, although he believed them superstitious nonsense. He longed for the night, when he'd slip out with one or two other students to workmen's homes to lead discussion groups about Marxism. Day and night he used every spare moment to read Marx and other revolutionary authors.

Gone were the times when he'd rise from a sickbed to do homework. He no longer cared about his marks, which fell steadily. What mattered was learning everything possible about Marxism and revolution. Despite the monks' vigilance, he had a collection of "illegal" books hidden around the school. These he'd read in lavatories, on back stairways, even during services, hidden under his prayer book. When he was caught, he went to solitary confinement in the Dark Room.

Instead of getting him to mend his ways, punishment made him more defiant. Once, while the principal searched his room, he continued reading a forbidden book as if no one was there.

"Don't you see who is standing before you?" the principal asked.

Soso rose from his chair and, rubbing his eyes, hissed, "I

don't see anything except a black spot in front of my eyes."

He was daring the authorities to punish him, and they didn't back down. In May 1899, at the age of nineteen, he was expelled from Tiflis Theological Seminary. His mother was heartbroken, but Soso was happy. At last he could set out on the path he'd chosen for himself. He became a professional revolutionary.

He found a job as clerk in the Tiflis Astronomical Observatory. Although the job paid very little, it covered his room and board. Anything left over went to books, his only real pleasure. He preferred to go about in the same filthy clothes, rather than do without a single book.

The year before his expulsion, some Marxists had gathered in the city of Minsk to found the Russian Social Democratic Party. Although the party was illegal, it quickly formed branches throughout the Russian Empire. Soso joined the Tiflis branch and, since he worked only a few hours each day, he had plenty of time to spread its propaganda.

He soon became known to the Okhrana, who opened a file on "the Pockmarked One," as they called him. One day, while he was away, the police came to his room to arrest him. Soso never returned to that room. After learning of the raid, he abandoned his job and possessions and began to live underground.

To live underground in tsarist Russia was to live as an outlaw. Soso learned that, in order to survive, he couldn't sleep in the same place for more than one or two nights; often he'd spend the night in the streets for fear his room was being watched. To throw the Okhrana off the trail, he carried false identification papers and constantly changed his name; Koba, David, Kato, Bars (Leopard), Ivanovich (son of Ivan) were just a few of his aliases. He became a master of disguise, using makeup to cover his pockmarked face, even occasionally dressing as a woman.

Most important, he learned that people were not always what they seemed. He came to distrust everyone, for a "friend" might be an Okhrana agent or someone who'd betray him for a few rubles. His years in the underground gave him a sixth sense about people that seldom failed. He could *feel* another person's weakness, or real strength of character. The slightest catch in the voice or change of expression set off a mental alarm—that person had something to hide.

Soso spent most of his time writing leaflets and speaking at workers' meetings. His message was always the same: form unions, strike, demonstrate to protest grievances. He knew that the authorities would meet demonstrators with violence, and this was exactly what he wanted.

Soso welcomed violence for two reasons: bloodshed was enjoyable to him personally as well as "educational" for the people. In his very first article, "The Russian Social Democratic Party and Its Immediate Tasks" written in 1901, he explained that demonstrations built revolutionary spirit. As demonstrators marched with their signs and chanted their slogans, they attracted "curious onlookers," including women and children. The police would then try to disperse them with clubs or, failing that, with gunfire. Some bullets would go astray, striking "curious onlookers." That was good, Soso believed, and the more the better. For in harming the innocent, the police turned today's "curious onlooker" into tomorrow's revolutionary. Individual lives meant nothing, so long as the revolution went forward.

The members of the Tiflis Social Democratic Party were not bloodthirsty. Basically decent people, their revolution was not meant to throw away innocent lives, but to achieve justice. They believed in comradeship, working together, and tolerating each other's faults.

But Soso Djugashvili was no comrade. Party members quickly realized that he wanted power for himself and would do anything to gain it. He formed his own little party within the party, demanding absolute loyalty from his followers. He spread rumors about the party's leaders, hoping to set one against the other. It was his first experiment in dividing the opposition, his favorite tactic in his later climb to power. This time, however, the tactic backfired and in 1901, after only two years in the party, he was ordered to leave Tiflis.

Bitter and lonely, Soso boarded the train to Batum to make a fresh start. Located on the Black Sea coast, Batum was a boomtown of oil refineries, railway depots, and factories. Employers might make fortunes there overnight, but not without suffering on the part of their workers. It, too, had its branch of the Russian Social Democratic Party, which Soso joined as soon as he arrived.

Early in March 1902, he helped organize an illegal strike at one of Batum's largest refineries. The owners, deciding to crush the strike immediately, fired four hundred men. A few nights later, Soso led three hundred workers in a protest demonstration outside the city jail. The police arrested everyone except the leader, who somehow managed to escape. Meantime, the governor of Georgia ordered troops into the city in case the demonstrations grew larger—a smart move, considering what happened next.

After his getaway, Soso made the rounds of the refineries to call for a monster demonstration. On the next day, March 9, two thousand men gathered from all over Batum. They were waving red flags and singing revolutionary songs when Soso's voice rose above the din, urging them on. "The soldiers won't shoot us," he cried. "Don't be afraid of the officers. Just go on and hit them right on the head, and our comrades will be freed."

The demonstrators were hit instead. As they neared the jail, an officer gave the order to fire. When the smoke cleared, fifteen men lay dead in pools of blood; another fifty-four were wounded and over five hundred were arrested. Soso came away without a scratch, and it was not due to luck. He was not the type to attack barricades with stones; his skin was too precious for *that*. During all his years as a revolutionary, he never appeared where there was real danger. He'd instigate others, give the marching order, and slip away before things got hot.

Three days after the shooting, Soso organized a "revolutionary funeral" for the slain. The funeral itself was a demonstration intended to show the government's cruelty and to raise the workers' anger to a fever pitch. With this in mind, he wrote a memorial to the victims. "All honor to you who have lain down your lives for the truth!" it said. "All honor to those whose brows are adorned with the crowns of martyrs. . . . All honor to your [spirits which] hover over us and whisper in our ears, 'Avenge our blood!' "

Not everyone took these words at face value. Many workers and Social Democratic Party members were angry at Soso for instigating the bloody demonstration and then calling for more of the same. People began to whisper that things weren't right with this young man. Perhaps he was an *agent provocateur?* Perhaps he was. But if so, he took care to cover his tracks. Years later, as dictator of the Soviet Union, he had any papers that might have shed light on his past destroyed, together with any people who knew about his early years as a revolutionary. All that is certain is that he was about to be booted out of another branch of his party when the police stepped in.

The police arrested him soon after the workers' funeral. The charges against him were never made public; he may not have been charged with anything, but arrested just to keep a troublemaker out of circulation for a while. After more than a year in jail, and without ever being convicted of a crime, he was sent to Siberia as a political exile.

Although he wasn't chained as a dangerous criminal would have been, the journey was not pleasant. The train chugged along at fifteen miles an hour, day in and day out, for an entire month. Soso, who'd never been out of the Caucasus before, was amazed as he watched the country gradually flatten out until the view was clear from horizon to horizon. Sometimes the prisoners were entertained by the native Siberian tribesmen. A horseman once challenged the train to a short-distance race and won by a mile.

Soso's place of exile was the village of Novaya Uda in Irkutsk province, some 4,000 miles from Georgia and 350 miles from the Chinese border. He felt stuck in the middle of nowhere and had to get away.

Within two months of arriving at Novaya Uda, in January 1904, he made a dash for freedom. Armed with a hunting rifle lent by a friendly grocer, he set out on foot across the frozen countryside. The wind wailed. Snowflakes hissed as they struck his face, hard as pebbles. He kept going until a bloodcurdling howl came on the wind. Wolves. It had been a harsh winter, and the animals were hungry. Suddenly he was attacked by ten wolves, snarling gray beasts with white fangs and eyes red as burning coals. Fighting for his life, he managed to drive them off and return to the village. There were no wolves ten days later when he tried again, and he was back in the Caucasus after many weeks of travel.

He would be banished to Siberia six times between 1903 and 1917. During these fourteen years, he spent a total of eight and a half years in tsarist jails and in exile. Each time, except for the last, he escaped easily. He always traveled alone, covering vast distances without leaving a trail. How he succeeded where so many others failed was never discovered. Rumors that he was an Okhrana agent, now helped to "escape" to improve his revolutionary standing, again surfaced. But without written evidence, this must remain a mystery.

Stalin's first wife, Ekaterina Svanidze. Below, a "mug shot" of Stalin taken around 1913, from the archives of the St. Petersburg Okhrana.

While hiding with his mother in Gori, Soso married the daughter of a family friend. Ekaterina Svanidze—"Keke"— was a gentle, pretty girl, religious, hardworking, and devoted to her family. No revolutionary, her husband's activities caused her endless worry. Iremashvili said that she would stay up nights alone, praying that he'd settle down to a steady job and a quiet home life. In 1908 she bore him a son, Yakov, whom Iremashvili later taught in elementary school. Unfortunately, the boy grew up without either parent. His mother died of tuberculosis soon after his birth, and his father left him to be raised by his aunts.

For the first time in his life, Soso had lost someone he cared about deeply. It hurt. Although an atheist, he gave her a Christian burial out of respect for her faith. At the graveside he pointed to the coffin and poured out his grief to Iremashvili. "This creature used to soften my stony heart. When she died, all my warm feelings for people died with her." Then he placed his hand on his heart and said: "It is all so desolate here, so unbelievably empty."

Never again would he allow himself to show such human feeling. After Keke's death, he took a new revolutionary name. At first that name was heard only in the underground, but eventually the whole world learned it. Little Joey Djugashvili was gone. In his place stood Stalin—"Man of Steel." From then on he prided himself on being as tough, and cold, and heartless as steel.

About the time he first went to Siberia, Stalin heard of the man who would change Russian history. Vladimir Ilyich Ulyanov, better known as Lenin, was short and bald, with bulging little eyes and a reddish goatee. He was born in 1870 into a prosperous family in Simbirsk on the Volga River, where his father was superintendent of schools. Vladimir's future looked bright, with a career in government service before him. Then, when he was sixteen, his world crashed in pieces. His older brother, Alexander, a student at the University of St. Petersburg, was hung for his role in a plot to assassinate Tsar Alexander III. From that day forward, the youngster, who'd worshiped his brother, became a revolutionary. After reading the works of Karl Marx, he vowed to lead the Russian revolution and set up the dictatorship of the proletariat.

Revolution became Lenin's only purpose in life. He'd sacrifice everything to that cause. He'd do without a normal home life; he and his wife, Krupskaya, as dedicated a revolutionary as himself, had no children and no home other than drab boardinghouse rooms. Lenin enjoyed playing chess and listening to music, but gave them up when they interfered with his work. He lived and breathed revolution. A fellow Communist said of him: "There is no other man in the whole world who is so wrapped up in revolution for twenty-four hours a day, who has no other thought but that of revolution and who even when he is asleep dreams of nothing but revolution."

Lenin's mind was as keen as a razor. Even when exiled in Siberia, he kept it sharp by constant study. His desk was always piled high with books on economics, history, and philosophy, which he eagerly explained to anyone who'd listen. As a speaker, he was in a class by himself. Unlike Stalin, who spoke slowly and for too long, Lenin was like a good teacher. He could boil down libraries of difficult books to a few simple ideas expressed in language ordinary people could understand.

If the desire for revenge made Lenin a revolutionary, it was his belief in final victory that kept him going despite everything. Lenin knew in his bones that Marxism held the key to history. Its "laws" were as true as any in science, as true as the law of gravity. He expected defeats. There would be hardships and disappointments. But in the end communism would be victorious. When his followers were downhearted, he wouldn't comfort them. Comfort was for weaklings, and they had to be strong. "Don't whine, comrades," he'd say through clenched teeth. "We are bound to win, for we are right." Such a man might be defeated again and again and still spring back, strong as ever, to continue the struggle.

When Stalin heard about him, Lenin was living with other Social Democratic refugees in Switzerland. From there he bombarded Russia with his writings, smuggled into the country by sailors and railwaymen. His articles in the Communist newspaper *Iskra—The Spark*—had a wide circulation, as did his most important work, the 1902 pamphlet *What Is to Be Done?* Lenin wrote easily, quickly, and clearly; many of his works are as exciting today as the day they were written. He wielded the pen as warriors wield the sword: to challenge the enemy, humble him, slay his ideas. Lenin's ideas created the Communist Party, led it to victory in the Russian Revolution, and were used to support the dictatorship Stalin developed, which exists down to the present day.

Lenin did not want the Social Democratic Party to seek a large working-class membership. A large membership was necessary for winning elections, but there were no elections or parliaments in Russia. Even if they were created, they should be ignored. Winning elections and passing laws to help improve working conditions was "reformism," trying to make capitalism work. That was like trying to raise the dead with mumbo jumbo, when what the workers really had to do was prepare for the revolution.

Lenin had no confidence in the people's judgment. He believed ordinary people were immature and, unschooled in Marxism, ignorant of their true needs. To show them the way, Lenin wanted a party of people like himself, devoted revolutionaries who knew they were right and would sacrifice everything to the cause. "Give us an organization of revolutionaries," he'd say, his eyes blazing, "and we will turn Russia upside down."

Lenin likened the party to a disciplined army under a general staff and a supreme commander—himself. It must be a secret army organized into "cells." Each cell would have a few members known only to each other, and only to the cell leader, who'd report to the high command. Each cell would agitate in factories, take over workers' discussion groups, and penetrate the armed forces. It would have an illegal printing press and gather weapons until the time came for an armed uprising. From time to time, delegates from the various cells would leave the country to attend a party congress where important issues would be discussed under the guidance of the supreme commander.

Lenin often used the word "democracy," but it had its own special, "Leninist," meaning. It did not mean that the people chose their leaders and held them accountable for their actions. *Democracy meant that the party ruled over the people in their best interests and for their own good.* And if the people disapproved? Well, that was just too bad. The party would force them to do what was right, force them to be free. Lenin's idea of democracy was, in fact, a polite term for his party's dictatorship. "The scientific definition of dictatorship," he explained, "is a power that is not limited by any laws, not bound by any rules, and based directly on force. The term 'dictatorship' has *no other meaning but this*—mark this well!"

Russian Social Democrats did mark his ideas well. Some believed that Lenin pointed the way to a happy future, others that he'd create a tyranny worse than any tsar's. Both sides clashed head-on during the 1903 party congress in London. After winning a vote on a secondary issue, Lenin's supporters called themselves "the majority," or *Bolsheviks* in Russian, while his opposition became known as *Mensheviks*, "the minority." From then on, the Social Democratic Party was divided, not about Marxism, but about its methods and the kind of Russia to be created after the revolution.

When Stalin returned to the Caucasus from Siberia in 1904, he found the Social Democrats arguing among themselves. The Menshevik group, the majority in Georgia—and most of Russia—were the same people who'd scorned him. The Bolsheviks, though few in numbers, were ruthless men like himself. Lenin became his idol, and his writings his own bible of revolution. He identified so closely with Lenin that fellow Bolsheviks jokingly called him "Lenin's left foot."

Russia had its first taste of revolution the year after Stalin returned from exile. The revolution grew out of an unnecessary war. In 1904, Russia and Japan quarreled over control of the Chinese territories of Manchuria and Korea. Tsar Nicholas II, never the cleverest of men, decided to settle the dispute by force. War, he thought, would expand his empire in Asia, while drawing his people's attention away from problems at home.

But the tsar and his advisers had underestimated their enemy, whom they mocked as "little short-tail monkeys" who'd scamper away at the sound of Russian cannon. Actually, the Japanese were a brave and resourceful foe who had more and better equipment than the Russians—and the training to use it. In January 1904, they sank most of the Russian fleet in a surprise attack on Port Arthur—Russia's main port on the Yellow Sea—then drove into the disputed territories. When the Russo-Japanese War ended in September 1905, the Japanese had made important gains on the Asian mainland, at the cost of thousands of Russian lives.

By then Nicholas II had more to fear from his own people

than from any foreign enemy. The war was unpopular among Russians, who couldn't understand why their sons had to die half a world away. Worse, the war had sent prices soaring and caused shortages of food, clothing, and other goods in the cities. The people had suffered enough. Something had to be done.

The people's frustration came to a head in St. Petersburg, Russia's first city ever since Tsar Peter the Great moved the capital there from Moscow in the eighteenth century. In January 1905, Father Georgi Gapon, a Russian Orthodox priest, decided to ask the tsar to protect the workers from their bosses. His plan was to lead a gigantic religious procession to the Winter Palace, the tsar's winter home, and give him a petition begging for his help.

The petition was written in the most respectful language. It asked Nicholas II to grant civil rights, limit the working day to eight hours, guarantee a daily wage of one ruble (about fifty cents), and legalize trade unions. The most important request was for an assembly to draw up a constitution for the Russian Empire.

People felt these requests were reasonable. They jammed meeting halls, listening with tears rolling down their cheeks, as the petition was read for their approval. They raised their hands, their fingers forming a cross, to show that their requests were sacred.

Tension grew as the procession day drew near. People knew they were taking a chance. Troops had been brought to the capital and their watch fires could be seen burning in Winter Palace Square, a vast cobblestoned area in front of the palace. They were simple, humble people. But they were people! They only wanted to live decently, as people should. And if the troops fired? God's will be done. They would sacrifice their lives for the holiest of causes, for *svoboda*, for freedom. "It is better to die for our demands than to live as we have lived until now," said one worker. "If I am killed, then do not weep," another wrote his wife. "Raise [our son] and tell him I died a martyr for the freedom and happiness of the people."

Sunday, January 9, 1905, dawned bright and cold. The air was crisp and calm without the slightest breeze. New snow blanketed the city, hiding the dirt in a mantle of white. "Bloody Sunday" was about to begin.

Father Gapon led some 200,000 people toward the Winter Palace. Men and women walked together, many carrying infants or holding toddlers by the hand. They had no intention of making trouble, let alone a revolution. Father Gapon had ordered that nothing should be done that might be taken as a provocation. Penknives were to be left behind; not even red handkerchiefs were to be taken out of pockets.

Father Gapon marched alongside a great gilded crucifix. Wherever one looked there were icons, holy statues, and pictures of the tsar. People sang religious hymns and "God Save the Tsar," the Russian national anthem. As the procession advanced, policemen took off their caps and stood at attention; onlookers crossed themselves as the icons passed.

When the head of the procession reached Winter Palace Square, its five entrances were barred by a human wall. Battalions of soldiers clad in long coats stood shoulder to shoulder, rifles at the ready. Squadrons of mounted Cossacks waited nearby with whips and heavy curved swords known as sabers.

Upon command, the troops opened fire. Hundreds of rifles spoke with an earsplitting CRACK! Cossacks spurred their mounts and plowed into the human mass, their whips swishing and sabers cutting into flesh. Among the first to fall was a white-haired old man carrying the tsar's portrait. Beside him fell a small child. Screams of terror filled the air, but the troops pumped volley after volley into the seething crowd. At last the people scattered, leaving behind two hundred dead men, women, and children and eight hundred wounded. The snow in Winter Palace Square had become crimson slush. Bloody Sunday was over.

Cries of pain and outrage echoed through St. Petersburg that night. Father Gapon wrote several letters to be read wherever workers gathered. He spoke not only for himself, but gave words to what people felt in their hearts. One letter began:

> Dear comrades-workers! The innocent blood of people has been shed. Let us store the feeling of anger and revenge toward the beast-tsar and his jackal-ministers. But have faith that the day will dawn when a host of workers more dreadful . . . will rise as one for freedom, for freedom for all Russia. . . . Let us . . . tear up all portraits of the bloodsucking tsar and say to him: BE THOU DAMNED . . . !

People did more than tear up the tsar's portraits. They seized anything that came to hand as a weapon: clubs, hammers, knives, bottles of acid, guns looted from gunsmiths' shops. The next morning, no one wearing the tsar's uniform was safe on the streets of St. Petersburg. The red banner of revolution appeared everywhere.

None of the illegal political parties led the Revolution of 1905. It was a genuine people's uprising, directed by elected committees, or "soviets." Beginning in St. Petersburg, workers in each factory elected delegates to the city soviet. The soviet acted like a military command, gathering arms, organizing resistance, and issuing orders through printed bulletins. The chairman of the St. Petersburg Soviet was Leon Trotsky, the son of a wealthy Jewish landowner in the Ukraine. Only seven weeks older than Stalin, he would later become his bitterest enemy.

The revolt spread like wildfire, and within weeks every large city had its soviet. It was as if the whole country had been waiting for the signal from the capital. Russian industry ground to a halt in a wave of strikes. Factory workers and shipyard workers, railwaymen and newspaper men, postal workers, shop clerks, and janitors, even the *corps de ballet* of the Imperial Theater, all went on strike. In the countryside peasants went on a rampage, always with the same cry: "Give us land!"

Gunrunners had a field day, smuggling pistols and explosives along underground networks that stretched clear to the United States. And these weapons were put to swift use. By the end of 1905, over 1,500 government officials had been assassinated, the highest ranking being the Grand Duke Serge, Governor of Moscow, blown to bits outside the Kremlin wall. The assassins had wide support in democratic countries, for, as Mark Twain wrote from America, "If such a government cannot be overthrown otherwise than by dynamite, then thank God for dynamite."

Nicholas II panicked. Fearing that the revolution was getting out of control, he granted the people civil rights and agreed to hold elections for a *Duma*, or parliament. His announcement cut the ground out from under the revolution. Most people abandoned the revolution, satisfied that they'd won and that Russia would be a better country. The holdouts were butchered by troops whose standing order was: "Don't skimp on bullets, and make no arrests."

Yet nothing had been won. The people soon found that "Bloody Nicholas" was also "Nicholas the Swindler." Within a year he dissolved the Duma and arrested its socialist members. "The Revolution is dead," cried Trotsky. "Long live the Revolution!"

He was right on both counts. Although the revolution had failed to overthrow the tsar, it did shatter the Russian masses' loyalty to tsarism. Until then, most workers and peasants had turned a deaf ear to the revolutionaries. They only wanted better lives, not to pull down the government under which they'd lived for generations. But 1905 changed all that. It convinced people of two things: that tsarism was evil and that it had to be overthrown by force. They, like Trotsky, knew there would be a "next time."

Although 1905 was a bloody year in the Caucasus, Stalin kept his distance from the fighting. Occasionally he addressed workers' gatherings, or wrote leaflets with such rousing titles as "Workers of the Caucasus, It Is Time to Take Revenge," but no one ever saw him where bullets flew.

Most of his time was spent as a missionary for Bolshevism. He traveled widely, defending Lenin's ideas and attacking the Mensheviks as fools and weaklings. He also disliked them because of the Jews in their ranks. Throughout his life, Stalin was an anti-Semite, a Jew-hater. He believed Jews were an inferior people; even when they spouted Marxist slogans they were really traitors to the working class. "The Jewish people," he announced, "produce only cowards who are useless in a fight."

Toward the end of 1905, a Bolshevik group in Tiflis sent him to a conference in Finland, then a province of the Russian Empire. Lenin, who had been unable to return to Russia in time for the revolution, had summoned the Bolsheviks to meet him there to discuss their next moves. Here Stalin and Lenin met for the first time.

At first Stalin was disappointed with his idol. He'd imagined Lenin to be a giant whose followers worshiped the ground he walked on. Instead he found a small, plain man in a rumpled suit whom anyone could approach. However, speaking with him convinced Stalin of his genius. Lenin, for his part, trusted the younger man. He made Stalin his lieutenant in the Caucasus; it was Stalin's first step up the ladder to supreme power in Russia. It was a decision Lenin would live to regret.

Stalin was especially helpful in the dirty tricks department. The revolution had not been crushed entirely, only pushed into the shadows. From here revolutionaries struck at tsarism, often with terrifying results. Between October 1907 and May 1910, revolutionary "hit squads" assassinated 4,322 government officials and wounded 4,465 others. Some of these were Stalin's victims.

Although the Social Democratic Party officially condemned assassination, Lenin favored anything that weakened the government, terrorism included. So did Stalin. He never pulled a trigger or tossed a bomb, yet he masterminded at least one major assassination. General Gryasnov, the military governor of the Caucasus, had whipped demonstrators and turned cannon against the workers' district of Tiflis. Stalin ordered a bomb thrown into his carriage.

Stalin was also skilled at "fund-raising." Revolutions cost money as well as lives. The Bolsheviks needed large sums of money for their underground operations and to support their full-time activists. Lenin wasn't fussy about where the money came from. A little was raised from legitimate sources, such as workers' contributions. More was contributed by the secret services of Japan, Austria, and Germany, who hoped to undermine Russia from within. A handsome Bolshevik even married an heiress to get at her money.

The largest sums, however, came from criminal activity, and here Stalin was a master. While hiding from the police, he met professional criminals, who joined his fund-raising operations for a share of the loot. He admired criminals, who, unlike some revolutionaries, acted rather than talked; while in power, he'd entertain guests in his private theater with gangster films. Stalin could have taught Hollywood's make-believe crooks a lesson or two. For example, he organized protection rackets in Tiflis and other Georgian cities. His henchmen would approach a shopkeeper and invite him to join their "protection service." If they refused or went to the police, they were beaten up and their property firebombed.

The best sources of funds were banks and post offices. Although Stalin never admitted it, he organized a series of daring holdups. One of his jobs became a sensation throughout Europe. One day in June 1907, his men were loitering near the Tiflis branch of the Imperial Bank. When a wagon delivering cash to the bank appeared, several bombs were thrown at it and the Cossack escort. In the confusion that followed, during which several Cossacks were killed and innocent bystanders wounded, the thieves made off with hundreds of thousands of rubles.

Stalin's operations not only enriched the Bolsheviks, but taught him how to manage violent, desperate men. His successes also made him more valuable to Lenin, who began calling him "the wonderful Georgian." No deep thinker, he nevertheless knew how to get things done—and God help anyone who stood in his way!

After the Tiflis robbery, Stalin moved to Baku on the Caspian Sea. Known as the "Black City," Baku floated on an ocean of oil. Oil bubbled through cracks in the ground and sometimes accidentally caught fire. The air, thick with oil fumes, echoed to the thump, thump, thumping of oil pumps. Blazing pillars of waste gases lit the night sky, casting an eerie glow.

Stalin became involved in the oil workers' unions and organized several large strikes. His days as a strike leader, however, were numbered. He was arrested for the second time in April 1908 and imprisoned in Baku for nearly a year, during which time fellow prisoners learned to fear him. True, the short fellow with the crippled arm was no match for most men in a fight. But he didn't have to fight to prove his dominance. His brooding, his icy stare followed by harsh words, showed that he was no ordinary jailbird.

His cold and unfeeling nature showed itself most during executions. Executions at Baku were carried out at night in the prison yard. On such nights the prison's air seemed charged with electricity. The prisoners couldn't sleep, but lay awake, shaking, even fainting, as guards dragged the condemned man screaming to the gallows. Not Stalin. Calmly, he'd curl up on his cot with a book or sleep while another human being was hurled into eternity with a broken neck.

Stalin took pleasure in provoking others into defying the prison authorities. But he never signed protests or took part in demonstrations. He always stood behind the scenes, egging others on and enjoying the result when the guards lashed out with clubs and rifle butts.

Another "amusement" was spreading rumors about fellow prisoners. Once, when a young Georgian was brought in, Stalin hinted that he was an *agent provocateur*. A gang of prisoners beat him senseless and would have killed him had guards not interfered. Another time he told a fellow Bolshevik that a police "informer" had to be eliminated. The man was stabbed to death, although no proof against him was ever found.

Stalin's best friends were not political prisoners but hardened criminals. Semyon Vereshchak, a revolutionary who did time with him in Baku prison, recalled years later: "[He] was always seen in the company of cutthroats, political blackmailers, robbers, and gun slingers." His closest friends were two brothers jailed for counterfeiting.

Stalin left prison for exile in Siberia in 1909 and escaped after only four months. Returning to Baku, he continued his revolutionary work while hiding out in the city's slums. The police took him again in 1910 and returned him to Siberia. After serving his time, he was released in June 1911, and ordered to stay out of Russia's large cities and away from the Caucasus. He disobeyed and snuck into St. Petersburg. He was arrested the day he arrived and sent to northern Russia.

By now it was 1912, the year Lenin deliberately set out to wreck the Social Democratic Party. During a conference in Prague, Czechoslovakia, then part of the Austrian Empire, he had the Bolsheviks set themselves up as a separate political party. The party was to be governed by a nine-member Central Committee headed by Lenin. Among the nine was Roman Malinovsky, whom Lenin considered a trusted friend. Little did he know that Malinovsky was an Okhrana agent who'd worked among the revolutionaries for years. Everything he learned about the Bolsheviks, and he learned a lot, went straight to Okhrana headquarters in St. Petersburg.

Stalin, meanwhile, had escaped again in February 1912. For the next two months he was always on the move, visiting the Caucasus, Moscow, and St. Petersburg. While in the capital, he helped found *Pravda—The Truth*—the Bolsheviks' official newspaper. Arrested soon after, he escaped for the fifth and last time in September. Toward the end of the year, he joined Lenin in Vienna, Austria, where he learned that he'd become a member of the Central Committee. In Vienna at that very moment was a bitter youth ten years Stalin's junior. Rejected as an art student, he'd been living as a tramp and was preparing to leave for Germany, where he hoped to make a new start. Although their paths would later cross with disastrous results, as yet neither Stalin nor Adolf Hitler knew of the other's existence.

His business completed, Stalin returned to St. Petersburg to continue his revolutionary activities. Yet from the moment he arrived, he was a marked man. Roman Malinovsky had alerted the Okhrana, who pounced at the first opportunity. He was arrested during a benefit concert for *Pravda*. Although he tried to slip out of the concert hall in a woman's hat and coat, his boots gave him away.

Since he'd escaped so many times before, the government sentenced him to four years in Kureika in northern Russia, above the Arctic Circle. Kureika was one of the tiny settlements that dotted a frozen land larger than the combined area of Germany, France, and Great Britain. For nine months of the year the land was plunged into darkness; during the remaining three months, the sun hung on the horizon, shining blood-red at midnight. Kureika itself stood on the banks of the Yenisei River, over a thousand miles from the nearest large settlement and six hundred miles from any rail line. When the Yenisei froze, steamboats couldn't move upstream, closing it as an escape route. Trying to escape overland meant braving ice fields, wolves, and police patrols with orders to shoot escapees on sight.

Stalin hated his prison without bars. For one used to Georgia's green hillsides and bright sunlight, Kureika was especially bleak. He wrote to Olga Alliluyeva, the wife of a friend in St. Petersburg, asking a special favor: "I shall be content if from time to time you send me a postcard with a view of nature. In this accursed country nature is reduced to ugliness—in summer the river, in winter the snow, and that's all the nature there is. I am stupidly homesick for the sight of a landscape, even if it is only on paper."

Unlike other exiles, who enjoyed visiting each other and discussing politics, Stalin kept to himself. He found that he had natural ability as a hunter, and soon his room was a clutter of nets, traps, and spears. He learned to get about by sled and handle a dog team. His only companion was a dog called

Tishka, which was all right with him. He didn't care for people and enjoyed talking to the dog. "He used to keep me company . . . during the long winter evenings. . . . I would sit reading or writing, and Tishka would run in from the cold and lie down, pressed against my legs, growling as if trying to say something. I'd bend down, ruffle his ears and say something like this: 'Well, Tishka, are you frozen? Warm yourself, now, warm yourself.' "

Stalin was in Kureika when the First World War began in August 1914. Although Europe was being torn apart, the war didn't touch him until late in 1916. The government, desperate for fighting men, began to draft political exiles into the army. Stalin was ordered to appear at Krasnoyarsk, a town on the Trans-Siberian Railway a thousand miles from his settlement. He made the journey with other exiles on foot and by reindeer-sled, arriving in February 1917. When the doctors saw his crippled arm, they excused him from military service.

We don't know how he took the news, but it couldn't have meant much to him. For within days of his arrival, newspapers arrived from St. Petersburg. There had been another revolution. Nicholas II was overthrown. The new government had pardoned all political prisoners. He was free.

STEPPING STONES
TO POWER

THE TRANS-SIBERIAN EXPRESS SPED WESTWARD CARRYING STALIN and other returning exiles. Their destination was the capital, now called Petrograd, since St. Petersburg sounded too German, and Germany was the enemy.

Stalin always remembered that journey. Crowds of local people met them at stops along the way. Learning that the train had revolutionaries aboard, they thanked God that at last "holy revolution, long-awaited, dear revolution" had arrived.

That revolution, like the one twelve years before, arose from military disaster. Once again much of the blame belonged to Tsar Nicholas II. His 1905 experience should have taught him that he was living on a volcano that could erupt any minute. Yet he wasted the years that followed. Instead of winning back the people's loyalty by improving their lives, he tried to turn Russia into a first-class military power. Billions of rubles were borrowed from foreign banks to rebuild his armed forces. By 1914 he'd convinced himself, and his French and British allies, that Russia was a great power. Like a gigantic steamroller, its forces would crush the enemy in any future war.

The "Russian steamroller" was a myth; no, a bad joke. True, there'd been improvements, but not enough to rank his country alongside a power like Germany. The outbreak of the First World War found Russia short of everything needed for twentieth-century warfare. Russian cannon were too few and too old. Russian railroads lacked the rolling stock to move millions of troops and their supplies. The supply of rifles was scandalous; when the war began, there were a million fewer rifles than frontline troops, the shortage growing to more than six million by 1917. Worst of all, Russia lacked brainpower in its top command. The minister of war bragged that he hadn't read a military book in twenty-five years. Knowledge wasn't necessary, for he believed in raw courage and cold steel—the bayonet. The Germans believed in explosives and bullets.

The Russian steamroller was no iron machine crushing everything in its path, but masses of men, mostly peasants, flung at the enemy. It was like tossing human beings into a huge meat grinder. At the Battle of Tannenberg in 1914, Russian troops moved through artillery barrages that sent domes of earth leaping skyward and shrapnel, steel splinters able to cut a man in half, zinging through the air. Once through the barrage, they faced machine guns in trenches protected by barbed wire. At the two battles of the Masurian Lakes in 1914 and 1915, tens of thousands of Russians were slaughtered in the swamps.

This wasn't war, but murder on a vast scale. By 1917 the Russians had lost a *minimum* of two million men killed, and another four million wounded, captured, and missing, the greatest slaughter ever recorded. In some battlefields bodies lay so thick on the ground that one could walk on a carpet of human flesh for a half-mile; in others the Germans had to remove mounds of corpses from in front of their trenches to clear fields of fire, before the next human waves hit.

Russia's morale, its will to fight, snapped. Frontline troops, sick of war, wanted only to go home. Civilians were miserable, frustrated, and angry. It seemed that everyone knew someone who'd lost a son or husband in the fighting. Prices skyrocketed, shortages worsened, and life grew harder each day. In every city people stood in line to buy the necessities of life. In Odessa on the Black Sea, they waited two days on line for a few drops of cooking oil. In Petrograd and Moscow, they lined up and waited throughout freezing nights for bakeries to open.

The revolution, when it came, surprised everyone, including professional revolutionaries, most of whom were in Siberia or out of the country. In Zurich, Switzerland, Lenin felt that he probably wouldn't live to see the revolution. Trotsky was in a tiny apartment on East 164th Street in the Bronx, New York, thinking about how to support his growing family.

The women of Petrograd set off the explosion. On February 23, 1917,* they began to protest the shortages of bread and coal. In the days that followed, factory workers downed tools and came out in support. They marched into the center of the city, shouting "Down with the war!" and "Down with autocracy!" But their cries for food were loudest. "Bread! Bread! Give us bread!" they chanted. Bakeries were looted and bakers roughed up. The strikes spread, and demonstrations grew larger, noisier, and more difficult to control.

The only thing Nicholas II could think of was to order his troops to fire into the crowds. That did it! Petrograd exploded in violence. People went on a rampage the likes of which had never been seen in the capital. Police stations were burned and policemen lynched. The courts were attacked and their records tossed from the windows, fluttering down like giant snowflakes. Mobs stormed the jails, releasing prisoners—political and criminal—and seized the city arsenal, taking whatever weapons they could find.

There was to be no replay of 1905. The bulk of Petrograd's 190,000-man garrison were new recruits, many from the city's own factory districts. The shootings upset them deeply, and, early in March, they began to talk things over in their barracks.

*This date is according to the old Russian, or Julian, calendar, which was twelve-thirteen days behind the Western calendar adopted after the Bolsheviks took power, making it March 8. Thus, what Russians call the February and October revolutions actually took place in March and November 1917, according to the new calendar. The Russian dates and names will be used here.

The discussions were loud and passionate. Some said a soldier's loyalty was to the army, his first duty to obey orders. Most disagreed. For them, it was one thing to kill Germans at the front, another to shoot fellow Russians, fellow workers. Soon companies, then entire regiments, joined the demonstrations.

The Duma also took a hand in the revolution. Although disbanded in 1906, the tsar later allowed it to meet, but under rules that made it impossible to check his power. Composed of educated, well-to-do people, the members of the Duma respected private property and wanted their country to have a real parliament. On February 27, the Duma defied Nicholas II and set up a provisional, or temporary, government until a constitution could be drawn up. Three days later, after senior army officers said they could no longer support him, the tsar resigned the throne and Russia became a republic.

But the Russian Revolution had only just begun. On the day the Provisional Government was formed, the Petrograd Soviet of Workers' Deputies sprang into being. Unlike the Provisional Government, the Soviet's members were workers. Although as yet few had heard of the Bolsheviks, most believed in socialism in one form or another. The Soviet decided to take matters into its own hands. Distrusting the Provisional Government, it called for soviets to be set up throughout the country and in army and navy units. More, its Order Number One told the military to obey only its commands.

Stalin arrived in Petrograd ten days after the tsar's fall. It wasn't the world he remembered. For one thing, he could walk about freely, since the Okhrana no longer existed. Everywhere the symbols of tsarism were falling. Portraits of the tsar were cut from their frames and stomped in the dirty snow. The imperial coat of arms was knocked off palaces, post offices, theaters, and other public buildings. Statues of Nicholas II and his ancestors were smashed to pieces or melted down.

Stalin also sensed a different mood in the city. A strange feeling of joy and foreboding, hope and fear, filled the air like electricity before a storm. The old order was gone, but no one really knew where the country was heading. Trucks filled with shouting, laughing soldiers sped through the streets at all hours. With the Tsar's fall, frontline units set up soviets and shot any officer who protested. Thousands deserted and streamed into the capital, uncertain why they picked this place at this time. Tens of thousands of criminals freed from the jails prowled the streets, often with guns bought from soldiers. Outside Petrograd, peasants drove away landlords and divided the land among themselves.

Meanwhile, the Provisional Government remained loyal to the Allies. Despite defeat, its members wanted to honor Russia's commitments to continue fighting until victory was won. Stalin agreed. As the only member of the Central Committee in Petrograd, he was the senior Bolshevik. Upon arriving, he joined Lev Kamenev, a fellow exile from Siberia, in taking over *Pravda*. Under their direction, *Pravda* supported the Provisional Government, insisting that Russian troops must defend their country as long as German troops obeyed their emperor.

The Germans, however, had other ideas. Things were going badly on the Western Front and would get worse once the United States joined the Allies, as was expected any day. Germany's only hope lay in transferring millions of troops from the Russian front to the West. And to do this they had to overthrow the Provisional Government, replacing it with one certain to make peace.

The German High Command chose Lenin for the job. They knew how he despised the Provisional Government; if it created a democracy in Russia, Lenin's hopes for a Bolshevik dictatorship would vanish like morning mist. German officials provided a special train to take Lenin across Germany to neutral Sweden, from where he'd enter Russia. They also secretly gave him large sums of money for propaganda and arms. Lenin was, in effect, a German agent sent to overthrow the Russian republic and engineer the defeat of his own country.

Lenin arrived at Petrograd's Finland Station, April 3, 1917, after an absence of ten years. He expected to be arrested as soon as he stepped onto the platform but was amazed at his reception. Fellow Bolsheviks met him with red banners, brass bands, and crowds of cheering supporters. He was unmoved. Unsmiling, his jaw set, he left the station and climbed onto an armored car to deliver his message. He delivered it loud and clear so everyone would understand. The Provisional Government, that capitalists' tool, was sacrificing Russia's young men in an immoral war. Russia must leave the war, then go on to shake the world to its foundations. "The Russian Revolution which you have accomplished," he cried, "is the start of a new era. . . . Long live worldwide socialist revolution!" Stalin quickly saw who was in charge. He repented his "error" with *Pravda* and backed Lenin without question from then on.

Lenin gained a more powerful ally when Trotsky arrived from America in May. While Lenin was to be the brain and voice, Trotsky would be the sword of the Bolshevik Revolution. Lenin, a genius at propaganda, hammered away with two slogans. The first, "Peace, Land, and Bread," had something for everyone: "Peace" appealed to soldiers fed up with war; "Land" offered the peasants their hearts' desire; "Bread" was for city workers worried about their next meal. The second slogan, "All Power to the Soviets," demanded power to the people. Both slogans were actually clever lies. Lenin never intended to let peasants keep the land they took or to give people freedom to vote against the Bolsheviks. Trotsky, on the

The Bolshevik Revolution in Petrograd. Above,
Trotsky's Red Guard use massed rifle fire to
overpower troops loyal to the Provisional Government. Below, Lenin addresses a May Day
demonstration in the early 1920s.

other hand, was a man of action. Workers remembered his role in 1905 and trusted him. He used his influence to become head of the Military Revolutionary Committee, the military arm of the Petrograd Soviet, and to form voluntary fighting units of "Red Guards."

Bolshevik headquarters in the Smolny Institute, formerly a school for aristocratic girls, became a hive of activity. As Red Guards stood watch outside, Trotsky spun the web of a vast plot. His plan was to stage a *coup d' état*, a swift overthrow of the government. Bolshevik fighters, aided by sympathetic soldiers and sailors, would strike at the government's nerve centers: offices, telephone exchanges, telegraph and post offices, banks, power plants, and railroad switching stations. The blow would fall simultaneously in Petrograd, Moscow, and other major cities, throwing the government off balance and preventing counterattacks. The main effort, of course, would be in the capital.

Timing was all-important. Alexander Kerensky, head of the Provisional Government, had promised elections on November 12 for a Constituent Assembly to draw up a constitution. If Kerensky could hold out until then, he might gain popular support. Lenin knew he must strike *before* the election. If the voters approved his coup, fine. If not, he knew what to do.

The uprising went like clockwork. Before dawn, on Wednesday, October 25, 1917, detachments of Red Guards set out on their missions. As Petrograders left for work, the crackle of gunfire was heard around the city. The Provisional Government collapsed. By early evening, only the Winter Palace was still held by a handful of loyal troops.

When Red Guards broke into the Winter Palace, they found themselves surrounded by undreamt-of luxury. Men in shabby coats and muddy boots stood on plush carpets, gazing upward at crystal chandeliers. The palace had twelve hundred rooms and corridors that stretched like avenues into the distance. Some soldiers became confused and began wandering about, searching for the enemy, soon becoming lost. One fellow heard a noise and, turning, saw a cavalryman bearing down on him. After firing a few shots, he realized that it was the reflection of a painting in a huge mirror. But the soldiers soon recovered from their shock, and, by early morning they had secured the sprawling palace.

Lenin was stunned by the easy victory. When he received the news, he raised a hand and turned it around his head. "You know," he told Trotsky, "it makes one dizzy." Then they looked at one another and smiled. They had reason to be happy. The capital of the largest country on earth had fallen to a handful of fighters in little more than a day. The cost: six killed and about thirty wounded. Moscow fell to the Bolsheviks a week later, after several hundred had been killed. Although no one could have known it then, these deaths were to be the first of millions.

Lenin set up a fifteen-member Council of People's Commissars to rule Russia until the Constituent Assembly met. Its president, naturally, was Lenin himself. Trotsky became commissar for foreign affairs. The commissar for national minorities was—J. V. Djugashvili.

We don't know what Stalin did to deserve this honor. His role in the Bolshevik Revolution is almost a total blank. Comrades saw him at Central Committee meetings, where he remained silent most of the time. He also addressed workers' groups, although not often, since he was sensitive about his Georgian accent. Beyond these activities, it is impossible to trace his movements in the weeks before the coup. He was, said one Bolshevik, a "gray blur."

Yet one thing is certain: in politics, Lenin never gave something for nothing. There had to be a good reason for taking the

Georgian into his government. Stalin's post may have been a reward for special undercover work during the coup. Or perhaps it was an investment in one who'd be useful in the future. Whatever the reason, Stalin was now part of the governing circle, and thus one of the most powerful men in Russia.

The Bolsheviks had overthrown the government. Now they had to conquer Russia.

Yet within days of the coup, they began turning the majority of the people against them. They started interfering with citizens' lives in ways the tsars never imagined. Lenin issued a flood of decrees aimed, he said, at "building socialism." Private citizens lost control of their property as he claimed nearly everything for the state. Banking became a state monopoly; citizens had to deposit all cash except what was necessary for their daily needs and withdrawals were limited to very small sums. Factories, mines, merchant ships, the oil industry, and all large businesses were nationalized. No one could hire others, and private trade, even for small shopkeepers, was abolished. A decree required peasants to sell food to the government at whatever price it set. Education practically came to an end as all church-run schools became state property.

These actions sparked resentment, but they were only the beginning. Elections for the Constituent Assembly were held as scheduled in November. The Constituent Assembly, the first and only freely elected parliament in Russian history, was a stunning rejection of Bolshevism. Only one in four delegates were Bolsheviks; the majority were Social Revolutionaries, a peasant party, Mensheviks, and Constitutional Democrats, or Kadets.

Lenin allowed the Constituent Assembly to meet on January 5, 1918, under the eyes of his Red Guards. The next day— away with the farce! When the session opened, a sailor announced that everyone must go home because "the guards are tired." Troops then drove out the delegates and shot down the demonstrators who gathered in protest.

Millions had supported the Revolution because they were hungry and yearned for freedom. Now, with all the force of a punch in the eye, they understood what "democracy" meant to Lenin. It meant governmental theft, dictatorship, and the rule of force—all because of the Bolsheviks' certainty that they'd found the way to paradise on earth. "Ought we to yield to the clamors of workingmen who have reached the limit of their patience but do not understand their true interests as we do?" asked Karl Radek, one of Lenin's henchmen. The answer was obvious. The Russian people had exchanged one autocracy for another. The old tsar was gone and a new, red tsar stood in his place.

But the red tsar was fighting for his life on two fronts. The Germans had cut huge chunks of territory out of western Russia and were menacing Petrograd. At the same time, civil war broke out. This war pitted the Bolsheviks, or "Reds," against the "Whites." The White leaders were not interested in restoring tsarism. Committed to the ideals of the February Revolution, they hoped to bring back the Constituent Assembly and establish an elected government. Generals such as Nikolai Yudenich and Anton Denikin in European Russia, and Admiral Alexander Kolchak in Siberia, drew thousands of volunteers to their cause.

The Whites also had foreign support. After the tsar's fall, Allied forces occupied the northern ports of Murmansk and Archangel to prevent the Germans from capturing the war supplies stored there. But when the civil war began, the Allies, fearing the Bolsheviks would make a separate peace, took sides. They reinforced their troops in northern Russia and sent other units—mostly Americans and Japanese—to Siberia to secure the Trans-Siberian Railway for Admiral Kolchak.

About 180,000 Allied troops served in Russia, a tiny force compared to the millions engaged on the Western Front. Although they saw little action beyond local firefights, they were (and still are) deeply resented by many Russians. Others, however, especially supporters of the Whites, agreed with the British statesman Winston Churchill, who denounced "the foul baboonery of Bolshevism" as "an animal form of barbarism" that had to be destroyed.

Menaced from all sides, the Bolsheviks took desperate measures. Since German armies were so near Petrograd, Lenin moved the capital back to Moscow in March 1918 to announce that Bolshevism had come to stay. He also changed the party's name to the Russian Communist Party and adopted a new flag. On that flag a hammer represented the factory workers, a sickle the peasants; they were crossed on a red background symbolizing revolution and the unity of working people the world over.

During the move to Moscow, Lenin sent a delegation headed by Trotsky to meet the Germans at the fortress city of Brest-Litovsk in Poland. He would have done almost anything, paid nearly any price, to end the war in the west. He had no choice; for if it continued, *both* Russia and the Communist Party were doomed.

The Germans had helped make the Bolshevik Revolution, and now they wanted payment. The price was high: parts of White Russia, Poland, Finland, the Baltic states—Estonia, Latvia, Lithuania—and the entire Ukraine; with these vast territories went over one-quarter of Russia's population and three-quarters of its iron and coal industries. Despite objections from some advisers, Lenin accepted the Treaty of Brest-Litovsk.

The treaty released two million battle-tested German troops for the Western Front. It also freed the Bolsheviks to deal with their enemies on the home front. Trotsky, now People's Commissar for War, became the father of the Red Army. His main problem was not finding troops but competent officers to lead them. There were plenty of experienced officers in Russia, but they had served Tsar Nicholas II. They despised the Bolsheviks and wouldn't have lifted a finger for them—if they'd had a choice. But Trotsky got their help by making them an offer they couldn't refuse. Thousands of officers from generals to lieutenants were ordered to report for duty in the Red Army. Those who refused wound up in forced labor camps, or face down in a ditch. Those who obeyed—and most did—had a surprise. Their wives and children were taken hostage and threatened with death if they didn't serve faithfully.

The Russian Civil War was a savage struggle where neither side expected or showed mercy. One atrocity bred another, as revenge became the order of the day. The Whites shot prisoners and the Reds announced that enemy wounded would be shot. If a village aided one side, every man, woman, and child was machine-gunned and every building burnt when captured by the other side. Lyova and Petya, two Bolshevik veterans of the Civil War, recalled their experiences:

> "They made our people dig their own graves and climb in and they made their comrades cover them with earth and trample on the graves," Lyova said. "But we knew as many amusing tricks as they did. And when there were not enough bullets, I strangled them with my own hands. Remember, Petya?"
>
> "Do I remember?" [Petya] snorted. . . .

The Civil War broke up families, turning fathers against sons, uncles against nephews. While visiting his native village in the Ukraine, the American writer Maurice Hindus met a young man, a Red, who recalled a wartime incident. He'd been leading a squad when fifteen peasants were brought in under arrest. They hadn't done anything wrong, but they had rifles and weren't Reds. One of them was his own uncle, a kindly man with seven children. When asked what they should do with the prisoners, he snapped "Shoot!" "My uncle," he continued, "burst into a wail. But I did not wait to hear his plea. I spurred my horse and dashed away to my next position." He spoke in a firm voice and without any sign of regret. Such incidents were typical, and those who'd lived through the Civil War were not surprised upon hearing them.

In addition to the White armies, the Bolsheviks were opposed by millions of people behind the lines. Branded "counterrevolutionaries," these people undermined the Bolsheviks in countless ways, large and small. Some cut telegraph lines, or blew up warehouses, or assassinated Bolshevik leaders. Lenin himself was not safe. In August 1918, the Social Revolutionary Fanny Kaplan shot him; he survived, but the bullet that lodged in his neck gave him pain for the rest of his life.

Still, one didn't have to fire a gun to be branded a counterrevolutionary. Hoarding food, talking against the Bolsheviks, or merely appearing to be prosperous was enough to bring trouble. Whole segments of the population—the nobility, ex-tsarist officials, clergy, industrialists, Cossacks—automatically became "class enemies." No longer would a man's *actions* determine his guilt—one of the basic principles of law. Now, under Bolshevik law, simply *who he was* was enough to condemn a man to death.

The Bolsheviks had a special way of dealing with their enemies: mass terror, or, to use its official name, the Red Terror. Terrorism, the use of violence to gain power, rule, and paralyze would-be enemies with fear, is a basic element in communist thought. According to Karl Marx, "Revolution is war, and war is founded on terror." Trotsky, in his book, *Communism and Terrorism*, wrote that by murdering one person, though innocent of any crime, the Reds would intimidate thousands;

therefore murder was necessary and good, because it furthered the revolution. Lenin turned these theories into action. His letters and orders urged his henchmen to use "merciless mass terror," calling his enemies "harmful insects" to be exterminated. This man, who couldn't keep cut flowers in his office because he couldn't bear to see them die, became the greatest terrorist of his time.

The Red Terror made punishment under the tsars seem mild in comparison. The tsars' secret police obeyed strict rules, which they broke at their peril. The Okhrana never took hostages or tortured suspects. No one could be executed without having first been convicted in a court of law; and the death penalty was used sparingly. In the eighty years before 1917, an average of seventeen criminals were executed per year. After the February Revolution, the Provisional Government abolished the death penalty except for army deserters; at this time the British and French were shooting scores of deserters each month.

Things were different with the *Cheka*. The instrument of Red Terror, Cheka was an acronym of the Russian for the All-Russian Extraordinary Commission for the Struggle Against Counterrevolution and Sabotage. As its head, Lenin appointed Felix Dzerzhinsky, the son of a wealthy Polish landlord turned communist. Under Dzerzhinsky the Cheka grew to over 250,000 full-time agents by the end of the Civil War. The Okhrana never had more than 15,000. It was bound by no laws except what was thought useful to the Revolution. "Chekists" were self-righteous men who felt themselves above common morality. "Ours is a new morality," declared the Cheka magazine, *Red Sword.* "To us everything is permitted, because we are the first in the world to take up the sword not for the purpose of enslavement and repression but in the name of universal liberty and emancipation from slavery." In other words, the

Cheka could torture and kill in the name of goodness and freedom.

Cheka methods, later studied carefully by Hitler's Gestapo, were utterly ruthless. There was no such thing as an arrest warrant; Dzerzhinsky's men had unlimited power of arrest. People were held in secret jails where they could be tortured by every means sick minds could invent. Prisoners were scalped, skinned alive, branded, rolled around in nail-studded barrels, or buried for half an hour in a coffin containing a rotting corpse. Sometimes prisoners were taken outside in sub-zero weather, stripped naked, and doused with water, becoming living statues of ice. Execution was a mercy after such treatment. Most were killed with a bullet in the back of the head, or "apple" in Cheka slang. The Cheka even had a song about apples:

> *Little apple, little apple, where are you rolling to?*
> *Are you rolling to the Cheka?*
> *Then you will never come back again.*

The Cheka was free of sex discrimination; women had as much opportunity to become executioners as men. Vera Grebeniukova of the Odessa Cheka, a beautiful girl, was said to have shot seven hundred prisoners in a ten-week period. We don't know what her victims' offenses were, but people were sometimes shot for strange reasons. One artist took a bullet in the head for "espionage"; that is, telling foreigners about the condition of Russian museums.

No person or group was safe from the Cheka and Red Terror. On Lenin's orders, Tsar Nicholas II, his wife, son, four daughters, three servants, and pet dog were shot and their remains thrown down an abandoned mine shaft. The Cheka, aided by Red Army units, exterminated about seventy percent of the Don Cossacks, who lived in the regions bordering the Don

River. The Bolsheviks were committing genocide, the systematic killing of entire groups—a policy Adolf Hitler would follow a quarter-century later.

Stalin had his first taste of power during the Civil War. Lenin admired his organizing abilities and began to use him as a troubleshooter. His first mission was to the south, where White forces threatened to halt grain shipments to Moscow and other industrial cities. Pressure was greatest around Tsaritsyn, "City of Tsars," situated on a bend in the Volga River.

Stalin set out in June 1918 with several hundred troops aboard two armored trains, rolling fortresses covered with slabs of steel armor plate and bristling with machine guns. "Be sure our hand will not tremble," he wrote Lenin. "We shall treat enemies as enemies deserve." Upon arriving, he organized special Cheka squads, and the jails were soon crowded with "enemies of the people," real or imagined. His orders were short and final: "Shoot!" Each night scores of victims were taken to a black barge anchored in the Volga, shot, and dumped overboard. As an added precaution, victims' families, friends, and coworkers were shot or sent to labor camps.

Stalin also interfered with the army defending Tsaritsyn. Although he had no military assignment, he began replacing officers on his own authority. Usually his choices had nothing to do with the officers' military ability. The men he removed owed their jobs to Trotsky; Stalin's replacements were loyal only to himself. Among these was the ironworker Kliment Voroshilov, who would later replace Trotsky as Commissar for War under the Stalin dictatorship.

These actions were the first steps in a plan to build an independent power base within the Red Army and Communist Party. Although Stalin never spoke of his plans, his actions showed that he was thinking about the future. A patient man, he knew how to bide his time until the right moment to strike. He didn't know when that moment would come, or how he'd use it, but he meant to become dictator of Soviet Russia. Already he'd marked Trotsky as the man to watch in any power struggle. He hated Trotsky's arrogance, his cleverness, his skill as a speaker and writer. And he hated him as a Jew.

At Tsaritsyn he began to chip away at Trotsky's authority. Not only did he remove Trotsky's men, he ignored his orders. On one of Trotsky's orders he scrawled: "To be ignored." That was a mistake militarily, for the Commissar for War was an able soldier, while Stalin knew little about planning campaigns. He once sent an untrained division into battle, which surrendered to the last man. Trotsky, sputtering with anger, fired off a telegram to demand Stalin's recall. Lenin did bring him back to Moscow in October 1918, only to assign him elsewhere. Early in 1919, Stalin was sent to help defend Petrograd, menaced by a White army under General Yudenich. This time he did better, recapturing a key fort that had been taken by mutineers.

By now the Bolsheviks' enemies were fighting a losing battle. Germany surrendered in November 1918, and the Allies began to pull out of Russia. Left on their own, the White armies crumbled.

By 1920, the only serious military threat came from Poland. The Polish nation, destroyed by its neighbors in the eighteenth century, had been restored after the First World War. Reborn Poland promptly invaded the Ukraine, claiming it as part of its original territory. The Poles drove all the way to Kiev, the Ukrainian capital, but no farther. Their path was blocked by Bolshevik forces under Mikhail Tukhachevsky, a twenty-seven-year-old military genius. Tukhachevsky easily routed the Poles and hurled them back over the border.

Lenin now decided to push this victory for all it was worth.

Poland, he said, was Communism's "bridge to the West." Both
the defeated Germans and the victorious Allies were exhausted
from the First World War and seemed ripe for revolution.
Here was a chance to change the world in a few weeks. Once
Poland fell, it would be easy to march to Berlin. Then, with
Russian manpower and German industry, he'd conquer the
world for Communism.

Tukhachevsky burst into Poland in July 1920 proclaiming,
"On our bayonets we bring peace and happiness to toiling
humanity! Forward to the West!" His troops, sure that victory
was theirs, shouted, "Give us Warsaw!" and "Give us Berlin!"
as they marched. But Tukhachevsky was advancing too fast.
His left flank became exposed. If the enemy suddenly swung
around, he might easily be taken from behind.

The job of guarding his flank was given to an army advancing
from southern Russia. Luckily—for the enemy—Stalin was
in charge of that army's political affairs. Instead of acting as a
covering force, Stalin, who wanted the "glory" of victory for
himself, raced ahead. Tukhachevsky was only thirteen miles
from Warsaw, the Polish capital, when the sky seemed to fall.
The Poles turned on his unguarded flank and won a smashing
victory. His army fled in headlong retreat, leaving behind
70,000 prisoners. Stalin had snatched defeat from the jaws of
victory.

Stalin's last military adventure came in February 1921 in his
native Georgia. When the Russian Revolution began, Georgia
declared itself an independent nation. Under Social Democratic leadership, Georgia became a model democracy. The
people were happy and supported their government completely.

Georgia's leaders, however, were Mensheviks, and for Stalin
that was the kiss of death. As a young man, Stalin had been
driven from Tiflis by Mensheviks. That hurt. Like the moun-
tainfolk with their vendettas, he never forgot or forgave an
insult. And now, after twenty years, he took his revenge. Agents

were sent to provoke riots in Georgian cities. When the police took action, he claimed they were persecuting Communists and sent troops to "restore order."

Georgians fought heroically, but without hope. Rather than surrender, many chose death in action or committed suicide. When the Red Army occupied Tiflis, its troops ran wild, looting, burning and murdering. After the conquest, Stalin addressed a mass meeting in the workers' section, where he'd once led discussion groups. He did not get a hero's welcome. An old woman, who'd once hidden him from the Okhrana, shouted: "Accursed one, renegade, traitor!" Others in the audience hissed and cried: "Murderer! Traitor! Renegade! Curses on you!" The Cheka went to work the next day and Stalin returned to the Kremlin.

By now Russia was feeling the effects of nearly seven years of world war, revolution, foreign invasion, civil war, and Cheka terrorism. The railway network had broken down over large areas of the country. Without transportation there was no coal to power factories or raw materials to turn into finished goods. Russia's cities were drab and cold, their citizens ragged, oppressed, and hungry.

Lenin himself was responsible for much of the hunger. We recall that in 1917 he'd ordered peasants to sell food to the government at prices set by the government. When they refused, he sent gangs of thugs into the countryside to seize crops at gunpoint. These measures backfired as peasants planted less and hid whatever they could for their families. In 1921 the government was forced to reduce rations for city dwellers by one-third.

That action triggered the last serious challenge to the Bolshevik government. It began as the Russian Revolution had begun: with strikes and demonstrations in Petrograd. Workers swarmed into the streets with banners reading:

Down with Lenin and horseflesh.
Give us the Tsar and pork.

In mid-February, two weeks after Stalin destroyed the Georgian republic, the disturbances spread to the naval base at Kronstadt, an island in the Gulf of Finland near Petrograd. Kronstadt's 16,000 sailors were heroes of the Russian Revolution. They had joined the people in deposing the tsar and helped Lenin overthrow the Provisional Government. They'd believed Lenin when he promised liberty, equality, and justice. Now it was clear that he really wanted to set up a dictatorship.

The disturbances in Petrograd were the last straw. Sailors poured ashore from their battleships, chanting, "Down with the Communists! Down with the Soviet Government! Long live the Constituent Assembly!" They drew up petitions demanding democracy, free speech, and free trade unions.

Lenin responded by ordering Trotsky and Tukhachevsky to drown the uprising in blood. That wasn't easy, since even Red Army troops saw justice in the sailors' demands. The first units sent into action refused to fire on their sailor-comrades. Cheka troops then shot the soldiers who spoke out and sent the rest across the frozen Gulf of Finland in a snowstorm. Each unit, as it advanced, was followed by Chekists with drawn guns, ready to shoot anyone who turned back. A proud Trotsky then announced that he'd swept Kronstadt "with an iron broom," that is, had nearly all the sailors killed.

Kronstadt convinced Lenin to restore some freedoms. Under his New Economic Policy—NEP for short—the government kept control of banking and key industries but returned small-scale manufacturing, trading, and agriculture to private hands.

Unfortunately, NEP came too late for the peasants. Already suffering from government grain thefts, they were pushed over the brink by bad weather during the 1921 growing season. Russia, which had been a major food-exporting country, suffered one of the greatest famines in history.

The famine of 1921–1922 shocked the world. Large areas of the Ukraine and North Caucasus, the nation's breadbasket, became a wasteland. Fields, untilled and covered with stubble, seemed to be moving, for they teemed with rats and mice searching for food. Hundreds of villages were peopled only by skeletons, while countless living skeletons wandered the roads in search of anything to eat.

"Anything" might be human flesh. Desperate people took to cannibalism to fill their bellies. "We hear," an official reported, "that women cut the arms and legs off a human corpse and eat them. Children who die are not taken to the cemetery but kept for food." Asked about the taste of human flesh, a Volga peasant replied that it was "quite good and does not need much salt."

In July 1921, the Bolsheviks swallowed their pride and appealed for foreign aid. America was the most generous. The American Relief Fund under Herbert Hoover organized a gigantic relief effort. In all, the United States Congress and private citizens raised $45 million, the equivalent of $450 million in today's money. Over 700,000 tons of food came from America to feed ten million people a day and tide the Russians over until the next growing season.

By 1922 the country was beginning to recover. The food shortage passed and people returned to work. The Bolsheviks' enemies at home and abroad had been defeated and the Party was firmly in control. In December, the country's name was changed to Union of Soviet Socialist Republics—U.S.S.R.*

*The U.S.S.R. is made up of states, or republics: Russia, White Russia, the Ukraine, Transcaucasia (the territory south of the Caucasus) and, after 1925, smaller republics like Kazakhstan, Uzbekistan, and Turkestan.

The Bolsheviks had won, but at what a cost! Not counting the two million who died in the First World War, between 1918 and 1922, Russia lost *at least* fifteen million people—two-thirds victims of the Civil War of 1918–1920, the remaining third fallen to starvation and disease in the famine of 1921–1922.

Worse was to follow. For as these tragedies unfolded, Stalin was preparing to take over the government of the U.S.S.R.

The government Lenin designed for the U.S.S.R. resembled a pyramid, narrow at the top and broadening toward the base. Supreme power lay with the Central Committee of the Communist Party, whose chairman, Lenin, made the most important decisions. Below the Central Committee was the Party itself, with its main offices in Moscow and thousands of cells scattered throughout the country. Every workplace had its own Communist Party cell. Cells were found in every government department, military and police unit, shop, factory, trading company, scientific institute, school, university, orchestra, sports team, theater, and dance company. The members of each cell, directed by a committee and an official known as a "secretary," saw that the leaders' orders were obeyed, disciplined workers, and distributed various benefits. If, for instance, you needed a larger apartment, you applied to the cell committee, which allocated living space for its "work unit." Such things as vacations and tickets to sports events were also distributed through the cell. Thus, whoever controlled the Communist Party's central headquarters in Moscow, controlled not only the Party, but the Soviet government and, through the cells, the entire population. And one day that man would be Joseph Stalin.

Stalin's work as a troubleshooter was only a sideline. He preferred to stay in Moscow, the center of power. Lenin liked having him nearby. Their offices were on the same floor and they met several times each day to discuss current business. Lenin often delayed a decision until he'd talked things over with Stalin.

Stalin enjoyed office work and had a talent for details. He'd spend countless hours at his desk, studying reports, writing memos, and puffing on his pipe. He spent so much time indoors that he developed the "Kremlin complexion," a grayish, pasty skin color.

Most Party leaders hated such work. Men like Trotsky found it dull, uncreative, and beneath their dignity. They preferred making fiery speeches and arguing about Marxist theory. That was a mistake—a *fatal* mistake. For when Lenin left the scene, whoever controlled the bureaucracy would also have the best chance of taking his place.

Here was the key to power! "Never refuse to do the little things," Stalin would say, "for from the little things are built the big." Beginning in 1918, he accepted positions others found boring, especially that of General Secretary of the Communist Party, which handled the Central Committee's day-to-day business. These positions gave him expert knowledge of the Party and government from top to bottom. While others busied themselves with affairs of state, he dealt with such questions as: Who should be chairman of the Party organization in Kiev? Should the head of the government department in charge of North Siberian lumbering be dismissed? Who should replace him?

When Lenin set up his dictatorship, there were not enough old Bolsheviks to run the country. Thousands of new people, many of whom hadn't fought in the Civil War, joined the Party. These people, hungry for jobs, were loyal to whoever helped their careers. And Stalin could hand out jobs! Thus, year by year, job by job, he built a following within the Party and government. Those who owed him favors were everywhere.

Some of Stalin's closest henchmen served in the "Special Section." That office, with its say-nothing name, was in reality his private police force. Its files helped Stalin keep tabs on thousands of officials. Its spies informed him about the daily activities of the Party's inner circle, especially who they met. Stalin himself could listen to their conversations. The inner circle were linked by a secret telephone system based in the Kremlin. Stalin had that system installed by a brilliant engineer, who added an eavesdropping device. Stalin then had him murdered, an example of how he always covered his tracks. Not even Lenin escaped his spies. Stalin had his telephone "bugged" and a spy planted in his household, a pretty secretary named Nadezhda Alliluyeva. Nadezhda, who we'll meet again, was Stalin's second wife.

Stalin took a keen interest in Lenin's health. In May 1922 a blood vessel burst in the Soviet leader's brain, paralyzing the right side of his body. Although he recovered within a few months, the handwriting was on the wall: Lenin's days were numbered. Trotsky, however, was the logical choice to succeed him. Lenin trusted him; he was a popular war hero and, as Commissar for War, had the army's loyalty.

Yet powerful politicians feared Trotsky might set up a military dictatorship. Grigori Zinoviev, Petrograd's Communist Party chief and one of Lenin's oldest allies, distrusted him. Zinoviev was a bully and a weakling, brave only against the defenseless. When workmen struck in sympathy with the Kronstadt sailors, he had them machine-gunned. He wanted his sons, aged eleven and thirteen, to be as brave as daddy. Each was given a revolver and told to shoot anyone hostile to Soviet power. Lev Kamenev, boss of the Moscow Party, despised Trotsky even though he'd married Trotsky's sister.

Stalin invited Zinoviev and Kamenev to join him in a triumvirate, or *troika*, Russian for the three horses that pull a sleigh. The troika was to block Trotsky and share power after Lenin's death. In accepting this offer, the two men completely misjudged Stalin. He seemed so dull, so slow-witted, that he could easily be managed by "clever" fellows like themselves. They imagined they were using Stalin when in fact he was using them. They'd made a pact with the devil. One day he'd make them grovel in dirt, begging for their lives, before having them shot.

The troika set out to undermine Trotsky at every turn. Zinoviev and Kamenev hurled angry charges against him at Party conferences. They spread rumors about him, which cost him precious time and energy to deny. Stalin's henchmen got rid of his supporters. Trotsky's allies suddenly found themselves sent on "urgent" missions abroad, or reassigned to hole-in-the-wall towns in Soviet Central Asia.

As Lenin recovered, he began to see his mistake in trusting Stalin. This was no comrade, but a selfish power-seeker who might destroy the Revolution. "This cook," he told visitors, "will concoct nothing but peppery dishes." Stalin became frightened, for he knew that Lenin was anxious to move against him. It would be the end of his career, the end of his life. He'd be a nobody.

A healthy Lenin could easily have clipped the Georgian's wings. But Lenin was a dying man. On December 16, 1922, he had another stroke that left him partially paralyzed. "God," as one Communist said, "voted for Stalin."

Lenin was in a panic. Although paralyzed, his mind was crystal clear. Stalin had to be stopped! No matter what it took, even if it cost his life, Stalin had to be stopped!

A week after the stroke, Lenin summoned his energies to dictate the famous "Testament" in which he warned against a split in the Party. Stalin, though, was his chief worry. "Comrade Stalin," he wrote, "having become General Secretary, has concentrated unlimited power in his hands, and I am not sure whether he always knows how to use that power with sufficient caution." A few days later he added: "Stalin is too rude, and this fault . . . [is] intolerable in the office of General Secretary. Therefore, I propose to the comrades to find a way to remove Stalin from that position. . . ." Knowing how the Bolsheviks operated, "removal" could only mean a bullet in the head.

A Party congress was scheduled for April 1923. Lenin, recovering rapidly, intended to use the opportunity to drop a bomb on Stalin. He would denounce him before the Communist world, ending his career in disgrace. But the bomb never fell. A few days before the congress, another stroke left him unable to move, speak, or write. This time the damage was permanent. A final stroke killed him on January 21, 1924.

Stalin was overjoyed. His office staff remembered years later that he never seemed happier than in the days following Lenin's death. At last supreme power was within his reach.

Stalin's public face, however, was one of deep sadness. Appointing himself chief mourner, he arranged a funeral worthy of an Egyptian pharaoh. The night before the funeral, he delivered the eulogy that millions of Soviet schoolchildren would learn by heart:

> We Communists are people of a special mold.
> We are made of special material.
> We are those who form the army of . . . Comrade Lenin.
>
> There is nothing higher than the honor of belonging to
> this army.
> There is nothing higher than the title of member of the
> party whose founder and leader was Comrade Lenin.
>
> The sons of the working class,
> The sons of want and struggle,

The sons of incredible privation and heroic effort,
They, before all others, should be members of such a
party.

In departing from us, Comrade Lenin enjoined us to
hold high and keep pure the great calling of member
of the Party.
We vow to thee, Comrade Lenin, that we will with
honor fulfill this thy Commandment. . . .

In departing from us, Comrade Lenin enjoined us to
guard and to strengthen the dictatorship of the pro-
letariat.
We vow to thee, Comrade Lenin, that we will not spare
our strength to fulfill with honor this thy Com-
mandment . . .

The next morning, as the funeral procession got under way,
everything that could make noise in the Soviet Union was
turned on. For three minutes the land echoed with an earsplitting mixture of clang, bang, jangle, hoot, toot, crash,
whistle, honk, swish, and roar.

Lenin in life was a menace to Stalin; in death he became
his closest ally. Stalin turned Lenin into a Bolshevik god and
made himself the god's high priest. One picture suddenly appeared everywhere—plastered over newspapers and on posters.
The photograph (on following page) showed the two men sitting together, happy in each other's company. Stalin, the picture implies, was Lenin's most devoted follower, while Lenin
loved Stalin as the son he'd never had. The picture was a fake,
made by pasting two photos together.

Stalin had Lenin's body mummified and displayed in a red
granite tomb, completed in 1929. He had every word Lenin
wrote collected and enshrined in the Lenin Library. A Lenin
Museum housed relics of the great man. Marxism no longer

Lenin and Stalin, in the photograph released shortly after Lenin's death. Though Lenin distrusted Stalin toward the end of his life, this photograph implied that they were on the best of terms, and that Stalin was Lenin's natural political heir.

existed; in its place Stalin put "Leninism," of which he was sole interpreter. Finally, he had Petrograd renamed Leningrad—"Lenin City"; other cities became Leninsk, Lenino, and Ulyanovsk.

Fooling the public was one thing. However, there was still an obstacle blocking his way to Party control: Lenin's Testament. If it became public, it might turn the Party against him. The big test came at the Party congress in May 1924. The Testament, sent by Lenin's wife, was to be read to the assembled delegates when Zinoviev came to the rescue. He persuaded the Central Committee to have it read during one of its closed meetings, where he defended Stalin. He was happy to report that Lenin's fears were unjustified, since Stalin was a good comrade after all. The Central Committee then voted to allow him to remain in office. Stalin breathed a sigh of relief.

The attack on Trotsky now swung into high gear. As in his prison days, Stalin used others to do his dirty work. He encouraged journalists to tear at Trotsky from every direction. Everything Trotsky said was analyzed and criticized. He was no Leninist, they said, but the father of wicked "Trotskyism." Stalin used the Party machinery to undermine him at every opportunity. Thousands of "Trotskyites" were removed from their posts and replaced by Stalin loyalists. Trotsky in time became a stranger in his own department. He was still Commissar for War, but ignored, like a piece of shabby furniture. The only thing for such a proud man to do was to resign.

Trotsky's defeat signaled the end of the troika. Stalin felt no gratitude toward those who'd helped him—nor to anyone else. Gratitude was not part of his nature. "Don't you know what gratitude is?" a fellow Communist once asked him. Stalin took his pipe from his mouth and said, "Oh yes, I know; I know very well: it is a sickness suffered by dogs." Zinoviev and

Lenin's funeral procession, which Stalin staged, passes beneath the Kremlin wall. Below, the leaders of the Communist Party after Lenin's death: (left to right) Stalin, Alexei Rykov, the nominal head of the Communist Party, Lev Kamenev, and Grigori Zinoviev. Stalin would later order the execution of all three on trumped-up treason charges.

Kamenev had served their purpose, and now he stripped them of their posts and their privileges.

At last they realized that Stalin was more dangerous than Trotsky. Meeting secretly with Trotsky in 1926, the three formed the "united Opposition" to Stalin. Soon an illegal printing press was churning out leaflets to be stuffed in Party members' mailboxes or tossed from rooftops. Opposition gatherings took place in factory cellars and workers' homes. Trotsky, who'd led millions of troops, was reduced to speaking in rooms with the furniture piled on the bed to make space for a few dozen listeners.

Stalin wasn't surprised. His "bugging" system revealed all the Opposition's plans. He let them go ahead, giving them enough rope to hang themselves. They did.

On the tenth anniversary of the Bolshevik Revolution, Zinoviev staged anti-Stalin demonstrations in Leningrad. "Long live the Opposition!" "Down with Stalin!" "Long live Trotsky!" protestors cried. At the same time in Moscow, Stalin viewed the anniversary celebration from atop Lenin's tomb. A group of Chinese Communist students came by under a *papier-mâché* dragon. Suddenly they lifted the dragon costume, threw Trotskyite leaflets into the air, and shouted "Death to Stalin!"

Stalin pulled on the rope—hard. The Oppositions' ringleaders were expelled from the Communist Party for staging an "illegal" demonstration. Humbled, Zinoviev and Kamenev begged for mercy and were readmitted.

But Trotsky was finished. In January 1928, four secret policemen came to arrest him. The man who'd organized the Bolshevik uprising, the father of the Red Army, had to be carried away kicking and biting. He was exiled to Alma-Ata in Soviet Turkestan and expelled from the U.S.S.R. in 1929.

———

Now Joseph Stalin could enjoy the celebration in Red Square that November 7. He had won, and this parade was to honor him, not the heroes of the past. He'd come a long way from battered child, rebellious seminarian, and political exile. Having beaten his opponents, he controlled the Communist Party and the Soviet state. Now he'd bend Russia's millions to *his* will, shaping them as *he* wished.

WORKERS' PARADISE

BOLSHEVIKS BELIEVED THAT THE "SCIENCE" OF COMMUNISM showed the way to human happiness. Unlike the great religions, which hold that true happiness can come only in the afterlife, Bolsheviks insisted that man needn't wait for the next world. After the Revolution, man could use communist science and human willpower to create a heaven on earth, a "Workers' Paradise."

A new type of person would be needed to fill that paradise. That person, the "New Soviet Man," would be a devoted Communist eager to sacrifice for Party and nation. But the Workers' Paradise and the New Soviet Man could not come about by themselves. Ordinary people were not supposed to be wise enough to decide important matters on their own. Communists believed that they needed a totalitarian system to push them along the right path.

Totalitarianism is no ordinary dictatorship. A typical dictator is like a gangster; he rules by force for his personal profit and that of his supporters. He interferes in peoples' lives only to protect himself and to exploit them. A totalitarian dictator wants more; actually, he wants everything. His goal is to remake his people by controlling all they do, think, and feel. In effect, they can have no privacy, no conscience, no life outside the system.

Lenin set up the first totalitarian system of modern times.*

---

*Sparta in ancient Greece was also a totalitarian state, but its power was limited to its small territory and by its rulers' lack of rapid communications and other means of enforcing their will.

Its foundations were firmly in place when Stalin took power. Stalin enlarged and perfected the system, spreading it to his East European satellites after the Second World War.

Stalin's Russia, no less than Imperial Russia, was a prison of the peoples. Its citizens had none of the liberties known in democratic countries. Russians could no longer voice an opinion, let alone criticize the government. Private discussion didn't exist; the police constantly spied on mail and telephone conversations. The Communist Party became the only political party; all others were destroyed, their leaders killed, and their members jailed. Freedom of assembly disappeared. No group could gather for any purpose without official permission and a policeman being present. This rule was strictly enforced, as several dozen youngsters learned when they attended an unauthorized concert. Those who weren't shot received ten-year prison sentences.

Soviet citizens could not move about freely in their own country. Under Stalin, everyone over sixteen had an "internal passport" for travel beyond their home area. Before setting out, you had to tell the secret police where you wanted to go and why. If your request was approved, a police officer stamped your passport, allowing one trip to one place for a set time. Every airport, railroad station, and dock had its secret police office, complete with jail cells. To buy a ticket, or to board, you had to show a validated passport. Whenever you stayed at a hotel, a policeman came around each night to see that your passport was in order. Being caught without permission to travel meant a longer journey—to Siberia.

Stalin also abolished freedom to move to, or even visit, a foreign country. Attempting to leave Soviet soil was treason, punishable by death. Only those on government business traveled abroad—and even then for very short periods of time. To make sure they returned, their families were kept as hostages.

There was no point appealing to the law if you felt wronged. Soviet law was whatever Stalin wanted. The courts served him and the Communist Party—which were the same thing—not justice. Instead of being treated as innocent until proven guilty, the mere fact of being brought to trial meant that everything had already been decided. Lawyers no longer defended private clients, but worked only for the government, which assigned their cases. The NKVD,* Stalin's new secret police, could search anywhere and arrest anyone. People could be jailed without charges, held without bail, questioned under torture, and executed without trial if that was in the interests of the state.

The NKVD backed Stalin's laws at every turn. One of these laws reveals a great deal about Soviet totalitarianism. It was the Family Law of April 1935, and it shocked the civilized world. This law made children of twelve and over liable to the same punishment as adults, including the death penalty for stealing a loaf of bread. No empty threat, this law was carried out in scores of cases. Moreover, the law made an entire family responsible for the actions of any one of its members. Thus, the relatives of a person who'd fled the country were held equally responsible and punished accordingly. Twelve-year-olds went to prison for failures of "revolutionary watchfulness"; that is, not reporting relatives guilty of crimes.

Yet fear has its limits. To create the New Soviet Man, Stalin also had to win people's hearts and minds. This meant two things: destroying old, "false" beliefs, and replacing them with new, "true" communist beliefs.

*The NKVD—People's Commissariat of Internal Affairs—replaced the Cheka in 1934. The NKVD was eventually replaced by the KGB—Committee of State Security—which is today the U.S.S.R.'s main secret police agency.

Religious beliefs headed the "false" list. Atheism has always been a basic tenet of communism. Karl Marx was a *materialist*, one who holds that everything can be explained in terms of matter. If you couldn't see and touch it, weigh and measure it, then Marx said it didn't exist. Thus "God" and "spirit" were lies taught by cheats and believed by fools. "Religion," he insisted, "is the opiate of the people." It is a drug to dull the miseries of overwork and poverty with promises of happiness in the next world. Humanity would never be free, never build communism, so long as it clung to religious myths.

Lenin agreed. "Every religious idea, every idea of God," he told Maxim Gorky, the famous Russian writer, ". . . is unutterable vileness . . . of the most dangerous kind. . . . Millions of sins . . . [and] acts of violence . . . are far less dangerous than the subtle, spiritual idea of God. . . ." Stalin, as we've seen, became an atheist while studying for the priesthood.

The Bolsheviks declared open war on God. Each campaign in that war was planned with the precision of a military operation. The war's objective was nothing less than ending the influence of religion in the U.S.S.R. It was an uneven contest; since there was no bill of rights to protect freedom of religion, the churches were defenseless against the government.

The offensive began with an attack on religious property, especially that of the Russian Orthodox Church, the largest in the land. Religious property was nationalized in 1918, when all buildings and lands were seized by the state. Beginning with Lenin, then at an increasing rate under Stalin, thousands of Christian churches, Muslim mosques, and Jewish synagogues were closed. In 1929, for example, 1,370 places of worship shut their doors; in 1937 the number was 1,511.

Hundreds of churches and monasteries were dynamited or pulled down for their building materials. Not even historic buildings were spared. Stalin personally ordered Kremlin churches dating back to the Middle Ages destroyed because they "blocked traffic." Buildings that survived were usually put to more "constructive" purposes than worship: turned into movie theaters, workers' clubs, machine shops, radio stations, warehouses, barns, and granaries. Atheist museums were opened in some of the more famous churches, the largest being Moscow's Central Antireligious Museum and Leningrad's Museum of the History of Atheism. In all cases the buildings were stripped of their religious ornaments, often artworks of great beauty. Ancient icons were burnt and wall paintings covered over with lime. Everywhere crosses disappeared from public view, replaced by red stars and the hammer and sickle.

Even when churches continued as places of worship, they could no longer summon the faithful. For centuries, bells played in the background of every Russian city and town. In Moscow, a city of churches, bells clanged at all hours of the day and night. Stalin ordered them silenced, as they "disturbed the workers." They were removed and melted down for their copper and tin. From then on, only traffic noises filled the air.

More important, those who preached the word of God were silenced. In the 1920s, thousands of the clergy died for their beliefs. During 1922 alone, 8,100 Russian Orthodox priests, monks, and nuns were executed. Their crimes were terrible in the eyes of the Soviets. Public Prosecutor Krylenko challenged several Leningrad priests:

> "Will you stop teaching the Christian religion?"
> "We cannot. It is the law of God."
> "That law does not exist on Soviet territory. You must choose. . . . As for your religion, I spit on it, as I spit on all religions."

Stalin broadened the assault on religion. Thousands of clergy and believers met death by cold and hunger in Siberian labor camps. In 1929 Stalin made a sweeping law to abolish religious teaching. The printing of religious books, newspapers, and magazines was outlawed. Religious instruction was forbidden unless done privately, and only for those over eighteen. It became illegal for parents to teach their children about God in the privacy of their homes. Doing so was "counterrevolutionary agitation," a crime that carried heavy fines and ten years at hard labor. Violators' children were taken away and raised by the state as orphans.

The meager civil rights allowed in Stalin's Russia were forbidden to believers. The 1929 law prevented them from running libraries, clubs, hospitals, and nurseries. Clergymen and their families faced discrimination at every turn. They were not entitled to medical attention, food ration cards, and state-built housing. Their children were barred from any school above the elementary grades.

These practices were not meant merely to punish believers, but to turn them into social outcasts. Thus children would be encouraged to break with their parents and others would see the price paid for such a "backward" idea as belief in God.

Stalin's war against God was aided by the League of the Militant Godless, founded in the mid-1920s. The league's aim was to "fight superstition" and it tried to discredit religious beliefs in any way possible. Its newspaper, *The Godless*, reached millions of readers each month with articles linking religion to capitalism and war. It held art exhibits which showed paintings of God, Jehovah, and Allah crushed beneath the wheels of Soviet industry. Its antireligious posters and cartoons portrayed clergymen as "black crows" and "filth." One of the crudest posters showed a pregnant Virgin Mary looking at an advertisement for a film on abortion, crying "Oh, why didn't I know that before!"

The League of the Militant Godless scorned holy days and religious festivals. Its speakers denounced Easter, "this foolish

A 1930 anti-religion poster. The caption reads,
"Proletarians be on your guard! The Black Crows
[priests] are flocking together to attack the USSR."

feast of nothingness," and discouraged the observance of Christmas, aided by Stalin's ban on the cutting and selling of Christmas trees. The league poked fun at God with antireligious films, musical comedies, and children's plays. Antireligious carnivals were staged during important holidays, the revelers carrying giant puppets mocking God, Christ, and Allah. Choirs sang familiar hymns, substituting words from revolutionary songs and coarse street ballads. In 1929, the league bought an airplane "to make war on heaven." It flew back and forth over Moscow, looking for God and challenging him to defend His sky.

The war against God also touched people in very personal ways. Before the Revolution, one's path through life had been marked by religious milestones, the sacraments of baptism, marriage, and the last rites. To further break the hold of religion, these services were taken over by the state and transformed into Soviet ceremonies. Now couples married at "red weddings," colorful affairs that omitted any reference to God. When children were born, they were named at the *Oktyabrin*, a ceremony honoring the Bolshevik Revolution. Children's names were no longer taken from the Bible or the Christian calendar of saints. The government issued lists of suggested names that praised communism, patriotism, and work. Among the new girls' names were: Revolutsia (Revolution), Barricada (Barricade), Konstitutsia (Constitution), Industriya (Industry), and Electrifikatsia (Electrification). Boys might be called Textile, Molot (Hammer), Serp (Sickle), and Ninel (Lenin spelled backwards). After the ceremony, a Party official congratulated the parents and gave them a "red baptismal" certificate. This welcomed the newborn to Soviet society with the words, "we greet you as a future worker and founder of the Communist social order. May the ideals of Communism henceforth form the content of your life as long as you live! . . . You shall march under the red flag! Long live the new revolutionary citizen/citizeness!"

Millions still held on to their faith, though for the most part they were older people, set in their ways from tsarist days. Among the younger generation, however, Stalin's antireligious campaign made real progress. By 1935, an estimated fifty percent of the population had fully or partially broken with religion.

A foreigner touring the U.S.S.R. that year reported on the state of religious beliefs: "I had to travel for miles in a Ford truck, since the churches in the immediate neighborhood were closed. The service was attended by a mere handful of people. I talked with the local priest and the first question I put to him was this: 'What is the future for religion in Russia?' Without a minute's hesitation the priest replied: *'There is no future for religion in Russia.'* "

Creating the New Soviet Man also meant replacing old beliefs with communist ones. This was no simple task in the U.S.S.R., where only four people in ten could read and write in 1917. The tsars had deliberately kept people illiterate, hoping to limit the spread of revolutionary ideas. Stalin favored literacy for the opposite reason: one who couldn't read couldn't easily be reached by propaganda.

Stalin made his country literate, perhaps his greatest achievement. He declared it everyone's patriotic duty to learn to read and write and to teach these skills to others. He spared no expense in building a network of schools in every city and rural district. Hundreds of thousands of teachers were recruited. In factories and Red Army camps, time was set aside each day for reading instruction. By the Second World War, at least ninety-five percent of the people were literate.

But *what* did they read? There was no freedom of infor-

mation in the Soviet Union. To Stalin ideas and information
were weapons in the struggle for power. They could either
undermine people's faith in the system or reinforce it. Thus,
he carefully regulated what people thought by regulating the
information they received.

Foreign ideas were kept out more effectively than under the
tsars. Stalin sealed the country's borders and had every person
and parcel thoroughly searched on entering. A few copies of
banned publications were kept in government offices for privileged readers, but otherwise it was illegal to own foreign publications. In some libraries, foreign newspapers and magazines
were made available only after offending articles were torn out.
Foreign radio broadcasts were jammed by transmitters ranged
along the country's western borders.

Russia's own publications were tightly controlled. Every word
in every book, newspaper, magazine, play, poem, film, ser-
mon, speech, scientific paper, and radio script had to be approved in advance by government censors. Usually they asked
that a fact be omitted here and a line toned down there, but
sometimes an entire piece was destroyed.

Stalin controlled every form of information and expression
at its source. In order to follow a career in a certain area, one
had to belong to the proper union. In communications, there
were unions for journalists and broadcasters. Performing artists
belonged to musicians', composers', dancers', and actors' unions.
Writers, painters, sculptors, and filmmakers had their own
unions. Each union had its own Communist Party cells, which
constantly evaluated members' performance and attitude.

Not being allowed to join a union, or being expelled from
one, was a disaster. Since the government owned all book-
shops, libraries, and printing presses, a disgraced author's works
were refused publication or pulled from shelves. Since all
theaters, dance troupes, record companies, orchestras and movie

studios were government property, an "unworthy" artist's works couldn't be performed. Since museums and galleries belonged to the government, the public never saw a blacklisted painter's works. Indeed, most of these works wouldn't have been created in the first place, since the government also controlled vital materials. An artist, for example, couldn't buy paints, brushes, and canvas without a union card. The same applied to music paper, typewriter ribbons, and other such items.

What determined whether one got into—and stayed in—a union was not a person's ability to speak truth or create beauty. One had simply to toe the government line. Stalin called writers and artists "engineers of the human soul." Their first duty was to mold the mind of the New Soviet Man. Journalists, for example, were not primarily interested in reporting the news: their first duty was to aid Stalin in accomplishing whatever goals he had at the moment. Said an editor of the newspaper *Izvestia* (*News*): "If it's printed, it's truth for us. We don't know and don't care about bourgeois notions of facts. We Soviet journalists are not just reporters. . . . We are in the thick of the fight, pioneers in the job of changing our country. If certain information retards this work, we would be crazy to print it. As far as we are concerned, it is then neither news nor truth." Thus, if a fact harmed the cause, it was a lie; if a lie helped the cause, it was the truth. Truth, actually, was anything Stalin said.

Similarly, Stalin drew no line between art and propaganda; they were the same to him. Their goal was to get people to think correctly and mobilize them in Stalin's service. Painters were to celebrate Soviet heroes and achievements. Architects were to design mighty buildings to symbolize the might of the state. Novelists were to create Communist heroes as models for ordinary people. Poets and musicians must inspire the people in the struggle against capitalism.

The most important task of creative people, however, was to glorify Joseph Stalin. They did their job so well that it was impossible for anyone not deaf *and* blind to escape Stalin's presence. No ruler in history, not even the god-kings of ancient Egypt, were so flattered.

Every day in every way Stalin's propaganda machine brainwashed the Soviet people into believing that he was the greatest person who'd ever lived. His name always had to be on people's lips. Whenever it appeared in newspapers and magazines, it was printed in larger letters than the rest of the text, just as God's name had been capitalized under the tsars. Every article and broadcast mentioned him several times, praising "the wise thought of Stalin" or "Stalin's great genius." At public gatherings, speeches began and ended with quotations from his writings. Mention of his name triggered wild outbursts by the audience. Everyone stood to applaud and cheer themselves hoarse. Not to demonstrate "love" for Stalin aroused the suspicion of the secret police, who attended all gatherings.

Merely thinking about Stalin drove some people out of their minds with joy. Alexis Tolstoy, a famous writer, gushed: "I want to howl, roar, shriek, bawl with rapture at the thought that we are living in the days of the most glorious, the one and only, the incomparable Stalin! Our breath, our blood, our life—here, take it, O Great Stalin!"

The dictator was honored in countless ways. Travelers rode over Stalin canals on Stalin bridges in Stalin cars on Stalin trains made of Stalinite, the hardest steel produced in Stalin steel mills. Vacationers visited any number of Stalin mountain peaks, or, if they favored the seashore, drove along Stalin roads to stay at Stalin hotels on Stalin beaches. During the Second World War, the Soviets' heaviest tank was called the Joseph Stalin.

Millions lived in places named in Stalin's honor. Tsaritsyn, renamed Stalingrad—"Stalin City"—became one of the bloodiest battlegrounds of the Second World War. Other cities and towns bore names like Stalinsk, Stalind, Stalinkan, Stalinsky, Stalinir, Stalino, Stalinbad, Stalinari, Stalin-Aul, and Stalinogorsk. Each of these, naturally, had Stalin streets, Stalin squares and Stalin parks; Moscow had its own Stalin district. Gori was especially privileged. The house he was born in became a shrine, enclosed in a glass bubble and decorated with a huge neon sign flashing "Glory to the Great Stalin!" in letters eight feet high.

Stalin was not satisfied just to be General Secretary of the Communist Party, although that was the basis of his power. His ego demanded grand titles, titles to make even kings blush. Just a few were:

> Great Leader of the Soviet People
> Wise and Intelligent Chief of the Soviet People
> Leader of the World Proletariat
> Best Friend of All Children
> Great Master of Daring Revolutionary Decisions
> Faithful Comrade-in-Arms of Lenin
> Transformer of Nature
> Great Strategist of the Revolution
> Supreme Military Leader
> Father of the Peoples
> Father, Leader, Friend, and Teacher
> Greatest Scientist of Our Age
> Granite Bolshevik
> Genius of Mankind

Last but not least, he was the Greatest Genius of All Times and Peoples.

Stalin's face was everywhere, stern but good-natured, following one with his all-seeing eyes. It was arranged in flowers on lawns, outlined in thousands of electric light bulbs, displayed on postage stamps, posters, postcards, and teacups. Main streets of towns were dominated by building-high pictures of the tyrant. His portrait often loomed above Moscow like a sky god, tied to an anchored balloon and illuminated with searchlights. A plane once towed a giant red banner bearing his picture, followed by a formation of planes spelling out "Glory to Stalin!" His portrait hung in every museum, public building, and schoolroom; 151 portraits and statues of him were counted in Moscow's Kazan Station alone. Portraits were serious business to him—and their accuracy was not the issue. He wanted to appear tall, with powerful hands, and heaven help anyone who couldn't deliver! Several portrait painters were shot for disappointing him.

Stalin's propaganda machine made him into a Communist substitute for God. Like God, he was all-good, all-wise, all-just, all-knowing, all-powerful. Poems credited him with being the creator of the world:

> O Great Stalin, O leader of the peoples,
> Thou who broughtest men to birth,
> Thou who fructifiest the earth,
> Thou who restoreth the centuries,
> Thou who makest the bloom of spring,
> Thou who makest vibrate the musical chords
>
> . . . .
> Thou, splendor of my spring, O Thou,
> Sun reflected by millions of hearts.

Another poet celebrated his supernatural powers:

> He orders the sun of the enemies to set.
> He speaks—and the East reddens for his
> friends.

If he tells the coal to turn white,
It will be as Stalin wishes.

Scores of songs, hymns, and choruses appeared each year to celebrate Stalin's greatness. One scholar counted over two thousand songs thanking him for blessings or mentioning his genius and superhuman powers. The list began with the Soviet national anthem:

We were brought up by Stalin, to be true to the people;
Toward great deeds of labor he inspired our hearts.

No other national anthem, not even that of Nazi Germany, praised one person, elevating him above the nation he ruled.

The propaganda worked, so much so that many ordinary people worshiped Stalin. People placed little plaster busts of the dictator where holy icons once stood in their homes. Stalin's picture hung alongside Lenin's on walls once decorated with saints' pictures. If something went wrong in their daily lives, or if a minor official gave trouble, a standard cry was: "If only Stalin knew!" But if Soviet chess players won an international competition, or aviators flew over the North Pole, or farmers had a bountiful harvest— then "Praise be to Stalin!" Even happy parents-to-be sang his praises. "Thanks be to Stalin!" cried a writer. "Thanks, for I feel well, thanks, for I am joyous, thanks. . . . My wife expects a child, [and] the first word that our child shall pronounce will be the name Stalin!"

The real Stalin, however, was nothing like the propagandists' image of him. The Soviets' heroic leader lived in constant fear. In time, most of his teeth became rotted stumps, because he was terrified of dentists. Heights sent him into a panic, and he only traveled by airplane once in his life, shivering all the way.

Stalin's greatest fear was of assassination. No ruler ever took such care in protecting his life. He surrounded himself with thousands of secret police guards, each of whom had been investigated many times. Every morsel of food was chemically analyzed before it came to his table. He always traveled in armored cars with windows of bulletproof glass two inches thick, a machine gun at his feet. And he knew how to use it, as well as the revolver he always carried. His private train had steel shutters that closed automatically at the flick of a switch and could withstand a siege of two weeks. His *dacha*, or country home, outside Moscow, had steel doors, barred windows, burglar alarms, electrified fences, and mine fields patrolled by guards with savage dogs.

During the mammoth May Day and November 7 parades, all windows fronting on the reviewing stand over Lenin's tomb were occupied by secret policemen. Certain streets were blocked off and people were shot when they blundered into these death zones. Every one of the million people, civilians and military, who marched past the reviewing stand was searched at least twice by security men before entering Red Square. None of the weapons carried by the parading soldiers were loaded; Stalin in any case wore a bulletproof vest. Secret police fighter planes cruised overhead with orders to shoot down unauthorized aircraft; once they downed three Red Army transports that had wandered off course. Stalin never took chances with his life.

The "man of the people" was the richest person in the Soviet Union. Not that his wealth was in the form of money. His salary was a thousand rubles a month, about forty dollars, less than the income of an American family on welfare. Yet he never spent his salary, which accumulated for years in his desk drawers. It wasn't that he was stingy, just that he had nothing to spend it on. Apart from some books and personal items, he owned nothing. Instead, he had the right to everything in the

Soviet Union. Ships, trains, and cars were his for the asking, paid for by the state. He enjoyed his *dachas* and had twenty of them in various parts of the country. Often they were built, torn down, and rebuilt time and again to satisfy his whims.

The Father, Leader, Friend, and Teacher was coarse and abusive toward everyone. Not even Lenin's wife, Krupskaya, a quiet, intelligent woman, was immune; he once shouted curses at her that can't be repeated here. Although usually very self-controlled, he occasionally had temper tantrums and threw stools at aides' heads. Nor was he above having people killed for the most harmless offense. During a vacation in June 1932, he was awakened by a blind man's Seeing Eye dog. He ordered master and dog shot instantly.

The Greatest Genius of All Times and Peoples amused himself in odd ways. When he was alone, he enjoyed looking at pornographic pictures, bought for him secretly in Western Europe by NKVD agents. In company, his idea of a joke was to humiliate others. During dinners with his staff, he'd roll pieces of paper into little tubes and place them on his private secretary's fingers, setting them on fire. The man squirmed in pain, but didn't dare remove the "candles," while his chief roared with laughter.

Stalin liked to get people drunk so he could laugh at them and, as an added bonus, study them off guard. He'd sit at the head of the table, ordering guests to drink more and more while water was substituted for vodka in his glass. The only person able to hold his vodka at such times was Nikita S. Khrushchev, the Party boss of the Ukraine—a talent that served him well. Occasionally Stalin went on all-day drinking bouts on his own. A foreign visitor witnessed one of these bouts:

> He drank glass after glass of wine, and after a while he began to dance. It was a gruesome sight, and the more

he drank the more fearful he looked. . . . He bellowed
with laughter, staggering and stamping around the cabin
completely out of time with the lovely music. . . . The
most frightening thing of all was that despite his drunk-
enness, he still seemed sober enough to observe my
reaction to his conduct. We spent the whole
day . . . with the drunken dictator, who seemed to me
more and more like some dreadful monster.

The Father of the Peoples was never a model family man.
He was not an attentive son, although he loved Ekaterina in
his own way. He gave her a tiny room in the palace of the
governor of Tiflis; it was all she needed, having been used to
much less. Yet she was lonely. Stalin seldom wrote to her and
saw her only three times in fifteen years. Although he vaca-
tioned in the Crimea, he never telephoned or invited her to
stay with him. On his rare visits she'd say, "What a pity you
never became a priest"; the fact that he never finished his
studies for the priesthood still hurt after so many years. She
died in 1936 in her eightieth year. Stalin was too busy to attend
the funeral, but sent flowers.

Stalin married his second wife, Nadezhda Alliluyeva, in
1919, when she was sixteen and he thirty-nine. There was
nothing strange about this; his bride was Georgian, and Georgian women usually married between the ages of thirteen and
sixteen.

Their marriage was not happy. Stalin was as crude with his
bride as with everyone else. He cursed her and seems seldom
to have shown affection. Nadezhda, however, was no shrinking
violet. She had a fiery temper and wasn't afraid to give him a
tongue-lashing. "You are a tormentor, that's what you are!"
she'd scream. "You torment your own son. . . . You torment
your wife. . . . You torment the whole Russian people!" Truer
words were never spoken.

Stalin had three children. Yakov, his son by his first wife, came to live with him when he became dictator. For some unknown reason he disliked his firstborn, a gentle, soft-spoken young man who got along easily with everyone else. Yakov, in Stalin's eyes, could do nothing right. He abused him with gutter language, calling him "My Fool" in front of others. Finally, in 1928 or 1929, Yakov tried to shoot himself. An understanding person would have seen the suicide attempt as a cry of pain. Not Stalin, who sneered: "Ha! He couldn't even shoot straight!"

Stalin had two children with Nadezhda: a son, Vasili, in 1921, and a daughter, Svetlana, in 1925. Vasili was a problem for his father from the beginning. When he was five months old, Nadezhda left him with his father while she tended to some chores. But the moment she turned her back, the baby began to cry. Papa Stalin looked into the cradle and, wanting to calm his son, puffed pipe smoke into his face. The cries became screams. Stalin then picked the infant up and stuck the pipe into his mouth. Vasili screamed as if he was being broiled. Stalin lost his temper. "There's a blackguard for you!" he growled, throwing the infant into the cradle. "He's not a good Bolshevik!" Vasili grew into a lazy, loudmouthed, good-for-nothing.

The only child for whom Stalin showed affection was Svetlana, and then only while she was young. During her growing years, he was a tender loving father. She remembers how there were always hugs and warm, tobacco-scented kisses from the pockmarked man who called her "Setanka" and "My Little Sparrow." When he was away, he wrote charming letters and sent gifts of fruit and candy. Here's a typical letter:

MY DEAR SETANKA!
I got your letter. . . . Thank you for not forgetting your little papa. I'm all right. I'm well, but I miss you.

Stalin's mother, Ekaterina Djugashvili, gives an interview to a Soviet newspaper reporter. Below, ten-year-old Svetlana and her "Little Papa" in 1935. Stalin was an affectionate father when Svetlana was young, although he eventually became cold and suspicious toward her.

Did you get the peaches and pomegranates? I'll send you some more if you order me to. Tell Vasya [Vasili] to write me, too. Good-bye, then. I give you a big kiss.

YOUR LITTLE PAPA

He always signed off with a kiss from "Little Papa" or "The poor peasant J. Stalin." But when Svetlana became older, and more independent, he treated her like everyone else.

Stalin might not have been the best of fathers, but he took a keen interest in young people. Not that they mattered in themselves—he cared nothing for them as individuals. They could live or die; it was all the same to him.

What mattered to Stalin was that the New Soviet Man should build the nation and conquer the world for communism. For this he needed children in vast numbers, which meant strengthening the family. After the Revolution, Lenin had made divorce as easy as mailing a form to a registry bureau in Moscow; abortion became a woman's right, obtainable free on demand. Stalin, however, turned back the clock. He made divorce so expensive as to be impossible for most couples; abortion was approved only in a medical emergency. Having children was a citizen's patriotic duty; women with more than five children were rewarded with medals and prizes.

Stalin looked to education to mold these children's minds— education he would control with an iron fist. No longer would schools train students for careers. The goal, Stalin said, was to make loyal Communists who'd fit neatly as cogs in the industrial-military machine he was building.

Teachers had to not only know their subjects, but also be staunch Communists, although not necessarily Communist Party members. No one could stand before a class without belonging to the All-Russian Union of Schoolteachers and passing difficult examinations in Marxist thought.

Classrooms were alike throughout the Soviet Union. Red hammer-and-sickle flags were displayed prominently. In front of the room, overlooking the scene like superfathers, were oversized portraits of Lenin and Stalin. Above the chalkboard was a saying of Lenin's in big, bold letters: "Study, study, and keep on studying."

All the children wore school uniforms; military-style outfits for boys, blouses and jumpers for girls. The purpose of the uniform was to train youngsters to see themselves not as individuals, but as members of a group. The group came first. Each row in the classroom was organized as an "academic team" whose members worked for the glory of the whole. Letting down your team was shameful for a budding Communist.

An important aspect of learning dealt with Communist morality. Lenin had discussed this subject in a famous speech of the 1920s. "Does Communist morality exist?" he asked. "Of course it does. . . . Our morality is entirely subordinated to the interests of the proletarian class struggle! . . . Whatever is useful to the revolution is moral; whatever is harmful to it is immoral and intolerable."

Lenin and Stalin both taught that the end justified the means, that anything could be done in a "good" cause. Children learned that personal morality didn't exist for Communists. Morality depended not on *what* was done, but on *who* did it and *why*. Honesty and loyalty, friendship and kindness, were moral only if they furthered the interests of the proletariat as defined by the Communist Party's leaders. "Everything," said Lenin, "that is done in the proletarian cause is honest."

Soviet schools taught the morality of the double standard, that what is right for me is wrong for you. When, for instance,

Stalin killed in the name of the Revolution, that was good. But it was wrong if capitalists killed revolutionaries. It was good that Stalin built up Soviet armed forces, because they protected the "Socialist Motherland" and furthered world revolution. But capitalists were "warmongers" if they built up their countries' military.

Children learned that lying and cheating were all right if they helped the Communist cause. So was murder, according to a widely used textbook of the 1930s: "If an individual . . . is dangerous to the revolutionary fight, you have the right to kill him. . . . The murder of an . . . enemy of the Revolution is a legal, ethical murder. . . ." Experience, however, teaches that ends really can't be separated from means, that doing evil in the name of good creates more evil. Murder can never be "right."

Standard subjects—mathematics, physics, chemistry, biology, literature, history—were always given a Communist slant. For example, atheism was promoted whenever possible. Such topics as "Why is it necessary to combat religion?" might be assigned for writing lessons. Children learned in history that Lenin and Stalin, but mostly Stalin, had led the Bolshevik Revolution; Stalin, not Trotsky, had created the Red Army and led it to victory in the Civil War.

Stalin worship, or the "cult of personality"—treating the leader as a god—was a basic part of Soviet education. From the moment their mothers left them for their first day of school, it was drummed into children's heads that Great Stalin, the atheist, was godlike. Youngsters were forever chanting "Thanks to dear Stalin for our happy childhood" and reciting a prayer to him:

Thou, our teacher, like the shining sun,
Dost open my eyes on heaven and earth,

Light up, my sun, shine in my window,
I see in thee the staff of life.

During school assemblies they sang *Glory to the Great Name of Stalin* and the hymn *Live Forever:*

Stronger than steel is thy name,
Brighter than sun is thy glory,
Sweeter than honey is thy word,
Live forever, beloved Leader.

Worship of Stalin might destroy children's love for their parents. A girl came home from nursery school one day and told her father, "You are not my father anymore."

"What do you mean I am not your father," he said, horrified.

"You are not my father anymore," she repeated. "Stalin is my father; he gives me everything I have."

Stalin filled youngsters' lives outside of school as well as inside. There was no such thing as young people following their interests on their own. All clubs, sports teams, and activities were illegal unless under the direct control of the Communist Party. Depending upon their ages, every boy and girl was expected to join one of three Communist youth organizations.

The youngest belonged to the Little Octobrists, named for the Bolshevik Revolution of October 1917. Little Octobrists' activities ranged from singing patriotic songs to excursions to monasteries, where they learned about the evils of religion.

At about the age of nine, children graduated into the Young Pioneers, remaining there until they were fifteen. Every school had its Young Pioneer cell, which organized student activities such as helping illiterates learn to read and leading revolutionary celebrations. Young Pioneer games were not childish pastimes, but played for Communist purposes. War games, for example, pitted the Red Army against the Whites. Another game was called "Getting the Revolutionary Literature Over the Frontier" and involved a team of Young Pioneers sneaking across a guarded capitalist border.

From fifteen to twenty-three, one belonged to the Communist Union of Youth, or *Komsomol.* The Komsomol was a training school for future Party members. Youths were watched carefully as they went about their duties. These duties might involve anything from leading a factory study circle to organizing demonstrations in favor of Stalin's policies. Komsomol boys also spent several hours each week at military drill and sharpshooting; girls learned first aid and how to prepare for air raids. At twenty-three, the best Komsomol members were invited to join the Communist Party; refusing the invitation meant risking your life during the Stalin years.

One's own life, however, was not the only one at risk. Every Soviet home had its NKVD spy. Children learned that Stalin wanted them to be vigilant. It was the youngster's duty to report "counterrevolutionary" activity, even if their parents were involved. Fathers and mothers went to jail for careless words spoken in front of their own children. Some died. In 1932, for example, Pavlik Morozov, aged twelve, reported his father for stealing a sack of grain from a state farm. Papa Morozov was promptly taken away and shot. A few days later, villagers killed the boy in revenge, only to be arrested and executed themselves. Pavlik became a hero for doing his "duty." The Palace of Culture of the Red Pioneers in Moscow was named in his honor and his statue was set up in his village. He is still held up as an example to Young Pioneers.

Stalin ran the Soviet Union from his private office in the Kremlin. There, in a gloomy room decorated only with portraits of Marx and Lenin, he decided the fate of millions. Although he listened to advisers' opinions, all decisions, and thus ultimate responsibility, was his own.

In the fall of 1928, Stalin decided to make his country the greatest military power on earth. This was a difficult task, since Soviet industry lagged far behind that of the West. To catch up, he made two decisions that would change the country forever. First, he decided on a rapid buildup of heavy industry: steel, machinery, oil, and hydroelectric power. This meant that old cities would expand enormously and new ones spring up, especially east of the Ural Mountains. Second, in order to feed the millions of new factory workers that would be needed, he decided to abolish the private ownership of land, turning farming into a government monopoly.

Stalin knew his plans would cause terrible misery. Since there was so little wealth available to buy machinery, and since foreigners refused to lend the Soviets money, the costs would have to come from the people. They would be overworked and underpaid and the "savings" plowed back into industry. Stalin was willing to have them pay any price for his idea of progress. The end justified the means for the "true" Communist. Individuals, living, feeling people, must be sacrificed to create the Workers' Paradise for future generations. He had no intention of asking people what they wanted. Why should he? He knew what was right and *he* had the power. The people would obey him—or take the consequences.

Stalin called his industrial program the First Five-Year Plan. Begun in 1928, it was to be renewed every five years until production had doubled and doubled again. Although the First Five-Year Plan fell short of its goals, it still made progress. Huge projects were completed. Tractor factories and machine shops rose at Stalingrad and Cheliabinsk. Steel mills lit up the sky at Magnitogorsk in the Urals, which grew from a population of zero to 250,000 in a few years. The Dneiper Dam, the largest in Europe, began to generate electricity. A new canal linked the Baltic with the White Sea. These projects, and others like them still to come, helped the Soviet Union survive during the dark days of the Second World War.

Yet success didn't come easily or cheaply. Since foreigners refused to sell machinery on credit, Stalin was desperate for money. To raise some of the cash, he turned to the "Nepmen," the private businessmen who'd prospered under Lenin's New Economic Policy. They were taxed heavily and their property seized without payment. Within two years private business had disappeared in the U.S.S.R.

The dictator, who'd used gangster methods against the tsar, used them again, only now on a larger scale. In 1929, large numbers of counterfeit hundred-dollar bills appeared all over the world. Investigators soon traced them to a small German bank secretly purchased by Soviet agents and used to pass millions of bad notes. Some agents even employed Chicago gangsters, associates of "Scarface" Al Capone, in their operations.

Kidnapping was another favorite technique. The NKVD would arrest Russians known to have relatives in the United States. They were then forced to write letters begging for money as "a matter of life and death." Others were allowed to leave the Soviet Union if relatives paid a passport fee in gold.

Gold, of course, was best of all, convertible into any currency. Those suspected of having gold were tossed into the "*parilka*" or "sweat room" by the NKVD. There, with the heat turned up to 113 degrees Fahrenheit and the ventilation shut off, hundreds of men and women were packed in so tightly that they had no room to kneel, let alone lie down. Most stripped in the unbearable heat, developing rashes from each other's sweat. They stood for days, sleepless, fainting, their feet swollen and bodies aching. The stench was nauseating, since there were no toilets. The guards fed them only salt herring, but refused to give them water when they became mad with thirst. The NKVD called these hellholes "gold mines." From them they drew a treasure of gold wedding rings, watches, tsarist coins, and tableware. Those who had no gold shouted their innocence until they died. But those who paid up were rearrested and tortured until they died or satisfied the NKVD that they had no more to steal.

Industrialization moved so fast and was often so poorly planned that disasters frequently resulted. Metalworking machinery bought with gold delivered to a factory before the roof was finished, rusted to junk in weeks. Overloaded trains derailed. Overworked mine equipment broke down, causing terrible accidents.

Stalin accepted no excuses for failure. He insisted that mix-ups, breakdowns, and accidents were caused by "wreckers," nonexistent Trotskyite agents. As a result, hundreds of innocent people became scapegoats for Stalin's own haste and ambition. Trials were held at which the accused were forced to confess their imaginary crimes. Often local Komsomol cells organized demonstrations to demand the harshest penalties for wreckers. During one trial in Moscow, thousands paraded past the courthouse, shouting "Death! death! death!" They had their wish. A railroad engineer was shot for overloading trains so as to wear out equipment. Three agricultural experts died for sabotaging the nation's rabbit-breeding program. Before mining engineer Andrei Kolodoob was executed, he was condemned by his son. The boy said in a letter to *Pravda:* "I denounce my father as a whole-hearted traitor and enemy of the working class. I demand for him the [death] penalty, and I reject the name he bears."

Stalin's decision to industrialize rapidly turned the Soviet worker into a state-owned slave. Rights taken for granted by workers in Europe and America didn't exist in the Workers' Paradise. Wages, for example, were paid not according to the hours worked, but on a piecework basis. Each worker had to wire so many light sockets or drill so many cylinders a day. Those who failed were fined or, worse, charged with sabotage; those who passed their quota received extra pay. Even so, they couldn't keep all they earned. Every paycheck had "voluntary" deductions for the Chinese revolution and similar causes.

Workers put in longer hours under Stalin than in tsarist times. Depending on the industry, they worked between forty-eight and sixty hours per week, Sundays included. Sunday sabbath, long held to be a day of rest and worship, was abolished. For Stalin that day was a link to hated Christianity. He replaced it with the "continuous work week" where every fifth day was a "free day" for one-fifth of the workers. Sunday became just like any other workday. Except for three national holidays, Soviet workers had no common day of rest.

The right to choose a job and quit if dissatisfied didn't exist in Stalin's Russia. The government assigned workers to their jobs, keeping them there or moving them about as it pleased. In 1931, for example, everyone who'd worked on a railroad in the past—engineers, firemen, track walkers, porters—was fired from his job and ordered back to the railroads. To change jobs one needed government permission. If granted, the permission, together with the new job, was entered in the worker's "Labor Book," his or her official job history papers. If you didn't get that permission, you were locked into your job whether you liked it or not.

Stalin's factories were really industrial prisons. Signs of the dictator's power were everywhere. Guards with rifles and fixed bayonets examined Labor Books at the gate. A "secret bureau," the factory's own office of the NKVD, spied constantly, arresting anyone for the slightest offense. Discipline on the job was enforced by terror. A few minutes' tardiness carried a heavy fine; being twenty minutes late three times brought ten years in a labor camp. Absence without a medical excuse, rarely given, could mean a firing squad.

Soviet workers had no defense against injustice. Every industry had its union, but like the artists' unions, they were only there to serve the state's interests. Stalin called them "transmission belts," since they transmitted government orders and saw that they were followed to the letter. Strikes were never tolerated. On the rare times they occurred, the NKVD always handled them the same way—with bullets. Once, workers in Leningrad's largest factory struck for more food. The authorities gave in and the strike ended peacefully. But in the weeks that followed, one by one the strike leaders were called to the secret bureau, only to disappear. The workers got the message and never struck again.

Even if husbands and wives worked overtime, their wages were seldom enough to meet basic needs. Most workers never had a decent home or privacy. Building materials were needed for the new factories, not to repair old houses or build new ones. As a result, houses fell into disrepair or became overcrowded. In Moscow, fifteen families often shared a tiny apartment; it was so tight that fistfights broke out over use of a stove or a broken toilet that stank to high heaven. Yet these people were lucky, compared to those in the new factory cities of the Urals and Siberia. There thousands of families lived in dugouts, damp holes in the ground with sod roofs and no plumbing.

Citizens couldn't walk into a shop to buy what they needed. There were shortages of everything, especially food, exported to pay for machinery purchased abroad. Each day was a struggle for enough to live on till tomorrow, when the struggle began anew. Most were thankful for a crust of bread, some sour cabbage, and a spoiled herring.

People got used to standing in line all night outside government shops in the hope of buying something—anything—when their turn came. Even if there were things to buy, money didn't go far. A pound of butter cost five days' wages; you worked two months for a pair of boots and four months for a suit of shabby clothes. You didn't complain about standing in line, because that was a serious, even a deadly, crime.

Yet life wasn't a struggle for everyone. Stalin did not believe in equality, declaring it "a piece of petty bourgeois stupidity." A clever man, he knew that he couldn't rule by terror alone. He needed loyal, efficient servants, and that required payoffs. Now in place of the old tsarist nobility, he put a "Stalinist" nobility. His nobles, of course, never used that term. They called themselves "leaders of the proletariat," but it was clear from the way they lived that they held ordinary people in contempt. They lived very comfortably, so long as Stalin found them useful.

The new nobility included Communist Party bosses, NKVD officials, factory managers, and favored writers, artists, and musicians. Nothing was too good for them! They had the finest houses, drove in limousines, and sent their children to special schools. Their servants shopped in the so-called "closed distributors," stores closed to all but the privileged few. There were no shortages in these stores. The finest imported foods, wines, and clothes were always available. Prices in closed distributors were low, so the noble's money bought up to thirty times more than a factory worker's.

Stalin's nobility enjoyed banquets and balls as lavish as any in tsarist Russia. NKVD chiefs had a club with thick carpets, gilt mirrors, and crystal chandeliers. During a masked ball, women guests wore low-cut evening gowns and their escorts tuxedos. Champagne and vodka flowed freely, served by white-gloved waiters. After having their fill, some drooling drunks shouted in chorus: "Thanks to Stalin for our happy childhood!"

Russia's peasants had no reason to thank Stalin for anything. For it was he who made them victims of the greatest crime in Russian history.

Peasant cooperation was vital to the success of the First Five-Year Plan. Stalin needed vast amounts of food to feed the growing work force in the factories and to export in exchange for machinery. Unfortunately, by 1929, Russia's 125 million *mujiks* in their seventy thousand villages were anything but cooperative. Mujiks, secure in their rights under the NEP, were the only Russians still outside Communist Party control. Independent people, they wanted to farm their own land in their own way, without interference from Moscow. They also wanted useful things—cloth, nails, boots, tools—in return for their crops, not paper money that bought nothing worth having. If the government couldn't provide the goods, the peasants would refuse to market their crops, growing only enough to feed themselves.

Stalin couldn't tolerate people looking after their own interests. It went against the very heart of socialism. Worse, such defiance would undermine the Five-Year Plan, maybe even trigger rebellion among the oppressed factory workers. There was only one thing to do: the Communist Party must control the entire economy. Just as private manufacturing and trade had been abolished, so must the private ownership of land. The peasants, whose desire for their own land had helped destroy tsarism, must be broken. Broken totally. Broken forever.

To achieve his aims, Stalin decided to create huge agricultural "factories." Every peasant family was to surrender its land, livestock, and tools to a collective farm, or *kolkhoz*. Never again would they be allowed to own private property other than the clothes on their backs. Barracks would replace their houses, and life would be ruled by the kolkhoz gong. The gong would wake them in the morning. The gong would summon them to meals in the common dining halls. The gong would call them to work. The gong would send them to bed. All decisions would be made by the state; they'd sow what the state ordered sown and harvest what the state wanted harvested. The state would supply seed and fertilizer and buy the crops at its own price. No peasant would be able to move to a new collective or leave farming. He would be a serf owned by Stalin instead of by a tsarist nobleman.

Stalin's first victims were the *kulaks*, Russia's most prosperous farm families, whom he considered capitalists. On December 29, 1929, a week after his fiftieth birthday, Stalin declared war with the slogan, "Liquidate the kulaks as a class!" It was not a matter of individual guilt or innocence. Kulaks were enemies of Communism, and it was therefore "just" and "necessary" to exterminate them for the good of the cause. Thus, some 1,065,000 kulak families, between five and six million men, women, and children, would disappear into the grave or into "special settlements" thousands of miles from home.

Stalin sent gangs of armed thugs into the countryside to deal with the kulaks. Well prepared for their mission, they'd been taught that kulaks weren't people but "bloodsuckers" and "parasites," their children "disgusting" and "lower than lice." They were to crush the kulaks, ignoring their pleas and their tears since, according to a well-known saying, "Moscow does not believe in tears."

Stalin's thugs spread over the land like a plague. The kulaks were not given the chance to join collective farms. Instead, everything they owned was taken away. Although it was winter, they were robbed of warm clothes, underwear, and boots; even hats were snatched off children's heads. Anyone who protested was shot on the spot or clubbed to death. The survivors were driven from their villages to live as best they could in caves, forests, and swamps. Most starved or died of exposure.

Millions of other kulaks were packed into unheated cattle cars reeking of cow manure and human vomit. Weeks later, and after many deaths along the way—mostly babies and young children—they arrived in remote areas of northern Russia, Siberia, the Urals, and Kazakhstan, a semidesert near the Caspian Sea. There they were dumped in special settlements, usually no more than signs tacked to poles in the middle of a wilderness. Using the few tools supplied by guards, they built huts for their families; in settlements on the Yenisei, kulaks lived in dugouts. In the spring they began farming from scratch, living on rations and planting seeds lent by the government. But everything had to be paid back after the first harvest, when they'd have to survive on whatever could be grown in such poor soil.

Russia's remaining peasants were mistaken if they thought that destroying the kulaks would satisfy Stalin. No sooner were the kulaks removed from a village then the peasants were "invited" to surrender their property and move to a collective farm. Protestors, however poor, were branded "kulaks" or "kulak agents" and deported.

The peasants were now convinced that Stalin would do anything to force them into collectives, which they rightly saw as slave colonies. They began to resist in every way possible. In thousands of villages mujiks vowed that, if they had to go to the collectives, it would be empty-handed. Homes, farm buildings, and equipment—plows, reapers, wagons—were smashed and burned by their owners. "We worked all our lives for our house, you won't get it," a woman screamed, flinging a torch through a window. "The flames will have it."

Farm animals were butchered wholesale as peasants ate up their wealth before Stalin could steal it. Wild feasts were held where people stuffed themselves, vomited, and stuffed themselves again and again. By mid-1932, they'd slaughtered over half the nation's livestock. Of Russia's 276 million farm animals, 152.5 million were slaughtered.

Peasants often expressed their frustration through violence, even against themselves. Whole families, determined to die free rather than live in collective farm slavery, joined hands and leaped in front of trains. Most, however, turned their anger against their oppressors. Any of Stalin's thugs foolish enough to go out after dark were found the next morning with their heads split open. Others were cut to pieces with sickles or doused with kerosene and turned into human torches. Open warfare erupted, especially in the Ukraine, where mujiks resisted collectivization with axes and pitchforks, shotguns and ancient military rifles. Not since Kronstadt had there been such a challenge to Soviet power; only now there were scores of Kronstadts—smaller in scale but just as intense—flaring across the land. And, like Kronstadt, they were drowned in blood.

Putting down these rebellions was work for professionals, not bands of Communist Party thugs. NKVD and Red Army units sped to the scene. In the battles that followed, poorly armed peasants defended themselves against tanks, artillery, and flamethrowers. Aircraft bombed and machine-gunned villages. Once a village was overrun, NKVD execution squads "mopped up" the survivors.

Resistance was so fierce that Stalin had to call a halt to his reign of terror. But the halt was only temporary, a breathing space while he prepared to finish the job. Stalin had decided on a final solution to the peasant problem. The centers of peasant resistance in the Ukraine and along the Don and Volga rivers were to be ravaged so completely that in future no one would dare question his decisions.

In July 1932 Stalin ordered all farmers in these areas, both those collectivized and independent, to deliver impossibly large quantities of food to government collection depots. Gangs of toughs were sent to each farm to make sure every ounce of food was delivered. Stalin's decree was a death sentence for millions of innocent people. It was the beginning of the greatest man-made famine in history.

Stalin's bands swept the land clean of food. By the fall of 1932, starvation and its related diseases were killing thousands of peasants each day. People mad with hunger tried to fill their stomachs with cats, dogs, rats, ants, earthworms, even lumps of clay. People ate the bark off trees, boiled leather belts, and cooked carpenter's glue. Some ate horse manure, which still had a few grains of wheat in it; others dug up dead horses and ate the rotting carcasses. And they ate other human beings. Cannibalism spread throughout the famine area, as people cut up and cooked corpses; some even killed and ate their own children. Officials reported awful scenes:

> The village was dead. Going up to one of the shacks we looked into a window. We saw a dead man propped up on a built-in Russian stove. His back was against the wall. He was rigid and staring at us with his faraway dead eyes. . . . We found more dead people in what had been their homes. Some bodies were decomposed. Others were fresher. When we opened the doors huge rats would scamper to their holes and then come out

Children in the Young Pioneers attend a trade union congress in Moscow in 1934. Below, some of the Bezprizornye (Homeless Ones), victims of the famine in the Ukraine, sleeping on a city street. Thousands of these orphans were rounded up and shot on Stalin's orders.

and stare at us. . . . Many of the houses were empty.
But to the rear the graves told a story of desolation and
ghastly death. . . . Signs were stuck up on these
graves. . . . [One sign read]: "I love Stalin, bury him
here as soon as possible."

Knowledge that there was plenty of food nearby sharpened
the peasants' hunger pangs. During the worst of the famine,
the U.S.S.R. exported millions of tons of butter, eggs, fish,
potatoes, and grain; grain shipments actually rose from 200,000
tons in 1928 to nearly 5 million tons in 1931. Stolen food
accumulated so fast that it often rotted before shipment. Mountains of grain and potatoes were piled in the open behind
barbed wire entanglements. Peasants who tried to take a few
handfuls for their families were mowed down by NKVD
guards.

Tens of thousands of orphaned children roamed the famine
areas, dirty, ragged, and crawling with lice. To survive, these
Bezprizornye—Homeless Ones—formed gangs with members
as young as five or six. They found shelter wherever they could
in open fields and doorways, in sewers and cemetery vaults.
Crime became a way of life for them, indeed, a necessity of
life. Anything not nailed down became fair game for child
thieves. They had been so brutalized that they had no qualms
about slitting a person's throat for a piece of bread, blood and
all.

The NKVD declared war on the Bezprizornye. Thousands
were herded into police-run orphanages, to be beaten and
brutalized further. The toughest were later recruited into the
NKVD as torturers and labor camp guards. Most, however,
were killed. As early as 1932, orders came from the Kremlin
to shoot the Homeless Ones and the starving youngsters who'd
come to the cities in search of food.

Stalin ordered these crimes, but he couldn't have carried them out alone. The Communist Party, NKVD, and Red Army commanders were just as guilty as their master. They'd closed themselves to human feeling. Mercy had become weakness in their eyes. Stalin knew best and must be obeyed absolutely. If he was wrong, then the guilt was his, not theirs, they thought. Lev Kopelev, a Communist Party activist who defected to the West, recalls:

> With the rest of my generation I firmly believed that the end justified the means. Our great goal was the universal triumph of Communism, and for the sake of that goal everything was permissible—to lie, to steal, to destroy hundreds of thousands and even millions of people, all those who were hindering our work or could hinder it, everyone who stood in the way. . . . That was how I reasoned, and everyone like me, even when . . . I saw . . . how they mercilessly stripped the peasants in the winter of 1932–3. I took part in this myself, scouring the countryside, searching for hidden grain. . . . With the others I emptied out the old folks' storage chests, stopping my ears to the children's crying and the women's wails. For I was convinced that I was accomplishing the great and necessary transformation of the countryside; that in the days to come the people who lived there would be better off for it; that their distress and suffering were the result of their own ignorance . . . ; that those who sent me—and I myself— knew better than the peasants how they should live, what they should sow and when they should plough. . . . In the terrible spring of 1933 I saw people dying of hunger. I saw women and children with distended bellies, turning blue, still breathing but with

vacant, lifeless eyes. . . . [But I did not] lose my faith.
As before, I believed because I wanted to believe.

Yet there were still a few who were shocked by what they'd
been ordered to do. The campaign was so heartless, so beastly,
that seasoned veterans of the Civil War balked. Some shot
themselves in disgust; others lost their minds. But only one
person dared protest to the tyrant's face.

When Stalin's wife, Nadezhda, learned about the famine,
she accused him of murder. He cursed her, insisting that talk
of famine was "Trotskyite lies." Unlike the 1921 famine, when
Lenin appealed to the world for help, Stalin tried to keep his
famine secret. Not a word about it was printed in the Soviet
press and it became a crime, punishable by three to five years
in prison, even to mention the word "famine." Nadezhda,
however, couldn't live with this lie. Helpless and broken-
hearted, she shot herself in November 1932. Her husband
took the suicide as a personal insult and a betrayal. He refused
to attend the funeral, nor did he ever visit her grave.

The famine ended, as it began, on Stalin's orders. By 1933,
he felt that the peasants had learned their lesson. From then
on they'd pay taxes as a percentage of grain actually produced,
rather than a fixed amount set by Moscow. Food was sent
to the stricken areas, along with city workers, students,
and Komsomols to help plant the spring crop. The 1933
harvest was one of the best on record, although people continued to die throughout the next year from the aftereffects
of famine.

Stalin was satisfied. True, the U.S.S.R. was no Workers' Paradise for the New Soviet Man. Still, he'd broken the hold of
religion, brainwashed millions, and brought the economy totally under Communist Party control.

These "successes" came at an awful cost in human misery and death. Scholars estimate that 14.5 million peasants died because of the man in the Kremlin, a number higher than the total deaths for all countries in the First World War. Although Stalin thought this tragedy "unfortunate," he also believed it necessary for the building of Soviet power. But then other people's lives never mattered to him; they were *things* to be used up as required. For as he used to say: "A single death is a tragedy; a million deaths is a statistic."

STALIN'S TERROR

AT FOUR O'CLOCK IN THE AFTERNOON OF DECEMBER 1, 1934, a young man arrived at the Smolny Institute, Communist Party headquarters in Leningrad. The building was a fortress with NKVD guards posted at the gate and in every corridor. Efficient men, they carefully examined every pass, even those of high-ranking officials they'd seen hundreds of times. But not today. When the young man showed his pass, they waved him through without searching his briefcase.

His name was Leonid Nikolayev and he had a pistol in his briefcase. A troubled man with many personal problems, he'd decided to kill Sergey Kirov. Besides being Communist Party boss of Leningrad, Kirov, aged forty-eight, was among those responsible for slaughtering the kulaks. Hard-driving and dynamic, Kirov was a rising star in the Communist world; delegates at a recent Party Congress had cheered him almost as loudly as Stalin.

Nikolayev made his way to Kirov's office and waited patiently in the hallway outside. No one challenged him, as the NKVD checkpoints were deserted. After a while, a door opened and a shot rang out. Workers who heard the shot came running, only to find Kirov dead, lying in a pool of blood, a bullet in his back. His assassin lay beside him, having fainted from the excitement.

Soviet newspapers reported the story under banner headlines. Describing the state funeral, they said how Stalin had loved Kirov. When he saw Kirov in his casket, he leaned forward, tearfully, to kiss his cheek. Eighty towns and villages

116

were named in Kirov's honor; one of the world's leading dance companies was renamed the Kirov Ballet.

Yet Stalin's show of love was just that—a show. We know today that Nikolayev had been encouraged and helped by agents of NKVD chief Genrikh Yagoda. And Yagoda, a lame, yellowish little man said to resemble a bat, never acted without his master's approval.

Stalin approved, for, despite all his power, he was frightened. He realized that countless Russians hated him—*had* to hate him for the misery he'd caused. Secret NKVD reports described the graffiti on walls of factory lavatories, savage scrawls about "Great Stalin." He read the latest jokes, like the one about the men whose car blew a tire. "A bomb under Stalin's behind wouldn't have made a bigger explosion," cried the driver.

Bombs under Stalin's behind! That wasn't funny, especially since leaders of the Opposition still resented their defeat. From exile, Trotsky thundered against the tyrant who'd betrayed the Revolution. Many ordinary Party members still respected Zinoviev and Kamenev.

"What if . . . ?" The question haunted Stalin. What if these men joined forces with the dissatisfied workers and peasants? What if Adolf Hitler, who'd taken power in Germany at the beginning of 1933, aided the Opposition in order to soften up the U.S.S.R. for an attack? What if the Japanese, already fighting in China, backed the Opposition in return for Soviet territory in the Far East? Although there was no evidence of such plots, that meant nothing to Stalin. This master of double-dealing knew that plots could take a long time to form and current threats might go undetected. And a tyrant can never be too careful.

Stalin decided to "purge"—wipe out—any threat to his power before it became serious. Proof of guilt had nothing to do with the purge, nor did proof of loyalty or innocence. His aim was not to punish, but to *prevent*. Anyone who knew anything that might be used against him, or who might lead the country in his place, or possibly oppose him in the future was doomed.

Kirov's murder was the opening move in the purge. Claiming that it was part of a vast plot, Stalin began arresting people in Leningrad. During the weeks that followed, more than a hundred former White officers were shot without trial; thousands of other Leningraders wound up in Arctic labor camps. Among them were the NKVD men who'd helped Nikolayev; the assassin himself vanished without a trace.

Stalin, however, was in no hurry. He moved cautiously, silently, like a snake stalking its prey. While Yagoda made his arrangements, Stalin announced the new Soviet constitution. Billed as "the most democratic constitution in the world," it guaranteed everything: freedom of speech and the press, freedom of assembly and the right to demonstrate, freedom from search and arrest without a warrant. The only problem was that it never went into effect, even for a day. It had been created to impress outsiders, non-Russians, many of whom naively accepted it at face value and became friendly toward "soviet progressivism."

Between August 1936 and March 1938, fifty-four ex-Party leaders were tried in three batches in the Moscow Show Purge Trials. These men had been Lenin's comrades, serving him faithfully in high positions; some, like Zinoviev and Radek, had returned with him from Switzerland aboard the "sealed train." Stalin had known them for years, especially Nikolai I. Bukharin, editor of *Izvestia* and author of large portions of his new constitution. Bukharin's family often spent summer vacations with the Stalins. To everyone's delight, Bukharin would fill the house with his pets—hedgehogs, garter snakes, a tame fox. His daughter, Svetlana, was a friend of Stalin's own Svetlana.

Suddenly such men were supposed to have turned traitor, or to have been traitors all their lives. They were accused of joining Trotsky in planning to murder Stalin, seize power, and give parts of the U.S.S.R. to foreign enemies.

These charges could never be proven in a real court of law; they were false charges, with no evidence to back them up. Yet Stalin and Yagoda, who managed the trials from behind the scenes, didn't need evidence. The accused would convict themselves. They would confess. What followed made the Soviet courts a circus and a mockery of justice.

It wasn't easy to get innocent men to confess to crimes punishable by death. Obtaining confessions took a lot of "persuasion" and time, often more than a year. But Stalin was determined to have his way no matter how long it took. When, for example, Kamenev refused to confess, Stalin called the NKVD man in charge of the case to the Kremlin.

"You think that Kamenev may not confess?" asked Stalin, his eyes boring into the man.

"I don't know," he answered.

"Do you know how much our state weighs, with all the factories, machines, with all the armaments and the navy?"

"Nobody can know that, Yosif Vissarionovich," he replied, puzzled. "It is in the realm of astronomic figures."

"Well, and can one man withstand the pressure of that astronomical weight?" asked Stalin.

"No."

"Now, then, don't tell me any more that Kamenev, or this or that prisoner, is able to withstand that pressure. Don't come to report to me," Stalin snapped, "until you have in this briefcase the confession of Kamenev!"

The accused, who'd approved of the Cheka's methods in

the Civil War, now learned the meaning of torture firsthand. Not that they were beaten, which would have left marks visible during the public trials. Instead, each man was put into his own private corner of hell. They were kept in solitary confinement for weeks on end. During the hottest summer months, the heat in their cells was turned up. Some prisoners were forced to stand for hours in front of floodlights that caused pounding headaches and permanently damaged the eyes. Food was kept to a minimum, and salty in order to raise a terrible thirst.

Mental torture, however, caused the worst pain. Bolshevik leaders might calmly sentence others to death with the stroke of a pen, but the lives of their own families were precious. Stalin knew this and used it against them. He insisted that their loved ones be put to death if they refused to cooperate. Bukharin, for example, was told that his wife and child would be strangled if he didn't confess. Eventually everyone gave in.

Once they surrendered, the showmen went to work. The Moscow Show Trials were actually theatrical performances. The actors—the accused—were given scripts to memorize. Stalin personally went over each script, cutting here, adding there, to make the confessions sound more convincing. Rehearsals were held in the actual courtroom to assure that everything went smoothly.

Nothing was left to chance. The trials were staged in a hall in the Kremlin, away from foreign reporters. The audience, admitted by ticket only, consisted of NKVD people in civilian clothes. To make sure everyone played his part, a special group of NKVD officers sat in the audience. The moment a defendant said anything wrong, they'd leap up shouting to drown out his words. The commotion would then give the chief judge an excuse to call a recess. A panel of judges, not a jury, heard the cases.

The defendants were no longer confident leaders, but gaunt, defeated men defended by lawyers in Stalin's pay. They faced Andrei Vishinsky, chief prosecutor and head of the law faculty of Moscow University. Vishinsky, thin and beady-eyed, wasn't interested in truth; he wanted blood. He enjoyed insulting men unable to defend themselves. He abused his victims, calling them "human garbage," "beasts in human form," "dregs," "scum," and "reptiles." He'd shout at the top of his voice: "I demand that dogs gone mad should be shot!"

The Soviet press and radio echoed Prosecutor Vishinsky. As instructed, they cried for vengeance, having already decided that the defendants were guilty. Thousands of Communist Party cells in factories added to the outcry. The workers at the Stalin Mine wrote to "the Great Leader of the great people, to the friend and beloved teacher, to the hope of toiling humanity, Joseph Vissarionovich Stalin" begging him to "track down and annihilate these wretches." Youth also screamed for blood. *Pravda* printed schoolgirls' poems demanding, "Let us shoot them like dogs!"

The defendants played their parts, knowing what failure would mean to their loved ones. They confessed, damning themselves while praising their tormentors to the sky. Kamenev addressed his children, warning them to learn from his fate and "work, fight, and if need be die under the banner of Stalin." Bukharin called Stalin "the hope of the world."

Only one man found the courage to throw away his script. Nikolai Krestinsky, an aide to the Central Committee, denied that he'd committed any crime. The Chief Judge, startled at such defiance, halted the trial for the day. The next morning, after many hours of "special treatment" by the NKVD, Krestinsky confessed to treason.

All the defendants were found guilty. Most were sentenced

to death by shooting; of the few who received prison terms, none survived the ordeal. Stalin gloated over his victims' deaths. During a dinner for NKVD officers, General Pauker imitated Zinoviev's last moments. As he was led out of his cell, he fell to his knees, pleading, "Please, for God's sake, call Joseph Vissarionovich." Stalin held his belly with both hands and shook with laughter.

No death pleased him more than Trotsky's. Since leaving the Soviet Union in 1929, Trotsky had led the life of a wandering exile. He moved from Turkey to Norway to Mexico, finally settling in a house in Mexico City protected by Mexican government guards. From there he denounced Stalin and planned for a Communist revolution across the border in the United States.

But the man in the Kremlin had a long reach. Stalin killed Trotsky by inches, slowly and with pleasure. Each day was torture, waiting for the next attempt on his life or word of the death of those near and dear. Everyone around him was under a death sentence. All seven of his former secretaries died mysteriously; one was found floating in a river, headless. Friends from Civil War days disappeared into forced labor camps. His first wife, divorced for thirty years, was sent to Siberia. Trotsky, the terrorist who'd approved of murdering the tsar's children, saw his own children murdered. His younger son, Sergey, an engineer with no interest in politics, vanished. His elder son, Leon Sedov, was killed by the NKVD in Paris. That broke his heart. He and his wife locked themselves in their bedroom for a week, seeing no one, eating nothing, just crying, crying, crying.

Death finally took Leon Trotsky on August 20, 1940, after the purge had ended. He was sitting at his desk writing a biography of Stalin when Ramon Mercader brought him an article to read. It was a hot day, but Mercader, an NKVD

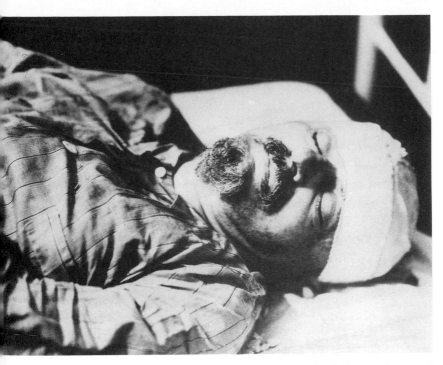

Leon Trotsky, the "sword of the revolution,"
brought down by an assassin in Mexico City,
1940.

agent, wore a coat. As Trotsky read the article, Mercader drew a mountaineer's ice ax from under the coat and smashed his skull. Mercader received a twenty-year prison term in Mexico, but refused to name those who'd put him up to the crime. That wasn't necessary. He received the gold-star medal of a Hero of the Soviet Union, and only one man could grant *that* award.

Meanwhile, the purge went forward like a runaway express train, crushing all in its path. No department of the Communist Party or Soviet government escaped. Party members at central headquarters in Moscow, Party secretaries in the republics and at the village level, officials of the Five-Year Plan, and Komsomol leaders were purged. Of the 1,966 members of the Party Congress in 1934, 1,108 were killed. The justice system, Stalin's tool for injustice, shared the same fate. Prosecutor Krylenko, who'd sent innocent priests to firing squads, was himself shot for treason.

The NKVD had a system for finding "traitors." A minor official would be arrested and pressured into confessing to some trumped-up charge. As part of the confession, however, he had to incriminate his superiors. They were then arrested and forced to incriminate those above them, and so on until a top official was arrested. With his fall, all his associates, friends, and their families were arrested, since Stalin didn't want to leave any future avengers. Thus, a few confessions eventually caught thousands in the dragnet. It was becoming dangerous to be a Communist Party member, as we learn from a popular joke:

"Knock knock."
"Who's there?"
"NKVD."
"You've got the wrong floor; the communists live upstairs."

Mass murder became a habit for Stalin, like smoking his pipe or drinking vodka. Every other day, sometimes more often, the NKVD chief sent death lists for Stalin's approval. During 1937 alone he received 383 lists containing some 40,000 names. He'd scan each list, then initial it. Often he added comments such as, "Arrest everyone" and "No need to check, shoot them." To the end of his life, Stalin approved at least two death lists each week, which meant that a day seldom passed without more blood staining his hands. He initialed the lists casually, without feeling, as if he were snuffing out vermin instead of human beings.

Stalin's henchmen used the purge to advance their own careers. Nikita Khrushchev, who would rule the U.S.S.R. from 1956 to 1964, ran the purge in Moscow and the Ukraine. Khrushchev supported Stalin enthusiastically. Great Stalin, he told a mass meeting, had ordered "enemies of the people" destroyed, and he was always right:

Stalin is our hope.
Stalin is our expectation.
Stalin is the beacon which guides progressive mankind.
Stalin is our banner.
Stalin is our will.
Stalin is our victory.

In the fall of 1936, Stalin took the purge in a new direction. Strange things began to happen at the NKVD. Yagoda was replaced by Nikolai Yezhov, a small, wiry man described as "a monster in human form." The NKVD knew too much about the Moscow trials and Stalin liked to keep his own secrets; besides, he didn't want his policemen to become too self-confident. So the sadistic Yezhov had been chosen to purge the purgers.

Yezhov made several hundred trusted officers, many from

Georgia, assistants to NKVD chiefs in Moscow and other cities. They were to help the secret police become more efficient, he said. Actually, they were to learn their chiefs' jobs so they could replace them at the right time.

When all was ready, Yezhov called the chiefs to a meeting in Moscow. He told them they were being sent on inspection tours throughout the Soviet Union. Each received a railroad ticket and orders to proceed to his destination immediately. None arrived. At the first stop outside Moscow, Yezhov's men boarded the train. Each officer was arrested, taken to a prison, and shot. General Pauker stopped laughing when they took him away.

Yagoda's sufferings didn't end so quickly. Arrested, he was tried for Kirov's murder, to which he confessed, along with being a German spy. Tearfully, he begged the court for mercy, but none was shown him. Shortly before his execution, he decided that God existed after all. From Stalin he deserved only gratitude for loyal service, he told a jailer. From God he deserved only punishment for his crimes. Stalin had betrayed him, so there must be a God, he reasoned.

Everyone who'd worked with Yagoda, or knew someone who'd worked with him, was a marked man. The NKVD owned several apartment houses near its Moscow headquarters. Those houses became filled with terror; one could *feel* it crackling in the air. Seeing their coworkers arrested, and living with fear, NKVD men broke under the strain and leaped from windows. Others stayed up nights, tensely waiting with drawn pistols. Sometimes a knock on the door of one apartment brought a suicide shot next door or across the hall. About 3,000 NKVD men died during the purge.

The next blow struck the armed forces. It began with a plot using the Gestapo, Hitler's secret police—an organization not easily fooled. Stalin had NKVD agents leak word that Soviet officers, including the Red Army's chief of staff, were planning to overthrow him. The Gestapo took the bait. Seeing a chance to cripple Russia in the next war, it forged several letters between its spies, Marshal Tukhachevsky, and Soviet commanders. The letters were then allowed to fall into Yezhov's hands.

Mikhail Tukhachevsky was Stalin's main target. After serving heroically in the Civil War, he'd become Red Army chief of staff. Thanks to Tukhachevsky, the Red Army had the largest tank force in the world and was the first to have regular paratroop units. Popular among the people, Tukhachevsky was seen as a possible rival to Stalin. Stalin, who blamed him for his own failure in the Polish war, now took his revenge. Tukhachevsky and others were arrested in June 1937 on charges of spying for Germany. At a secret trial, the forged Gestapo letters were used as proof of their guilt. All went to the firing squad.

Their deaths opened the way for a massacre of Soviet officers. During the next year, the Red Army lost 3 of its 5 field marshals, 14 of its 16 army commanders, 60 of its 67 corps commanders, 136 of its 199 division commanders; the Red Navy lost all 8 admirals. In addition, the army lost half of its officer corps, 35,000 men ranging from colonels to company commanders. Some died for ridiculous, almost comical, reasons. During a war game, a general Lukirsky attacked the U.S.S.R. from the west. His plan was so good that his army—the "Blueforce"—could only be stopped outside the capital. Lukirsky was shot for "letting the enemy get to the gates of Moscow." In one year Stalin killed more Soviet officers than Hitler would during the entire Second World War.

The purge touched even those closest to Stalin. Two of his brothers-in-law were shot, probably because they knew too much about his early life and crimes. A third brother-in-law, a Red Army general, died of a heart attack. But he may also have been killed; for as the NKVD used to say, "Any fool can commit a murder, but it takes an artist to commit a good natural death."

Abel Yenukidze and Sergo Ordzhonikidze, fellow Georgians who'd been Stalin's friends since 1900, found that they'd never really known him. Yenukidze, a favorite drinking companion, was arrested and shot after a pleasant evening alone with Stalin. One day Stalin sent Ordzhonikidze three NKVD men, a doctor, and a pistol. He'd recently spoken against the purge of the Red Army and Stalin took any criticisms as a betrayal. The NKVD men gave Ordzhonikidze the choice of suicide or execution. He said good-bye to his wife, went into the next room, and shot himself. The doctor wrote "heart failure" on the death certificate.

The purge began its last, and deadliest, phase in the spring of 1937. Until then it had claimed thousands of victims from among the ruling classes. Now it began to claim millions of ordinary citizens who had nothing to do with politics.

Stalin knew that these people, let alone their families, hadn't committed treason and probably never would. He also knew the Russian proverb: "Fear has big eyes." He believed that arresting suspects for real crimes wasn't as useful as arresting the innocent. Arresting someone for a crime that could be proven would allow everyone else to feel safe. And safety bred confidence, and confidence drew people together. Fear, however, sowed suspicion. It built walls between people, preventing them from uniting against his tyranny. And the best way to create fear was to strike the innocent. Millions of innocent lives were, to Stalin, a small price to pay for safeguarding his power.

Creating fear was easy. The NKVD had blanketed the country with informers. Like the secret police itself, informers were everywhere. An informer was stationed in every apartment house in every street in every Soviet town. Every office, shop, factory, and army barracks had its informers. He or she could be anyone: the janitor, the bank teller, the nice lady across the hall—or your best friend. Informers sat in the theaters, rode the trains, and strolled in the parks, eavesdropping on conversations. Although there is no way of checking, it was said that one person in five was a stool pigeon.

People became informers for various reasons. Some were professionals trained and paid by the NKVD. Most, however, were ordinary people. A person might be called to NKVD headquarters and "invited" to become an informer. It was dangerous to refuse and, once involved, impossible to stop. If you didn't denounce enough "traitors," you automatically came under suspicion yourself.

Stalin's system brought out the worst in people. Citizens were encouraged to denounce each other for money and benefits. Stool pigeons received one-quarter of each victim's property, a tempting bonus for underpaid workers. If one wanted a neighbor's apartment or a coworker's job, you reported him to the NKVD for some crime, real or imagined.

What might seem ridiculous to citizens of a democracy cost people their lives in Stalin's Russia. A bootblack, for example, was denounced for using poor polish in order to create dissatisfaction with Soviet-made shoes. A woman went to prison for saying that Tukhachevsky was handsome. After the death of his father, a boy found a copy of Lenin's Testament in one of his books. Foolishly he showed it to some friends, among them an informer. They were arrested and sent to Siberia. A man was arrested for "smiling in sympathy" while drunken sailors in a café told anti-Soviet jokes. Sentence: three years at hard labor.

Informers were most eager to report offenses against Stalin.

His name, like God's, could not be taken in vain. A half-literate factory worker enjoyed writing his own name in his spare time. Since blank paper was scarce, he used newspapers. A neighbor found a newspaper with his name written across the face of the Genius of Mankind. The worker got ten years in prison, as did the poor fellow who shot his air rifle at a newspaper page without noticing Stalin's picture on the other side. A typesetter went to his death in Siberia for accidentally misprinting Stalin's name, another for dividing it at the end of a line.

One man nearly lost his life for acting sensibly during a meeting. When Stalin's name was mentioned, the audience burst into applause. For three minutes the applause continued. People's hands began to ache, but no one dared be the first to stop. They knew there were informers in the room. Five minutes! People looked at each other sideways, wondering if they'd have to applaud until they collapsed. Ten minutes! At last someone stopped applauding and sat down. Instantly, everyone followed his example. The NKVD came for him the next day. He'd committed a grievous crime, punishable by ten years in Siberia, his examiner explained. But for some mysterious reason he was freed with only a warning: "Don't ever be the first to stop applauding!"

Victims were usually arrested in the wee hours of the morning. Imagine being startled awake at 4:00 A.M. by a clanging fire alarm. Now imagine people pounding at your door with fists and pistol butts. Opening the door, you find yourself facing five or six men in brown uniforms and blue caps. At that moment you realize that you've lost control of your life.

The bluecaps hustle you inside and order you to dress. Then, as you and your family sit shivering with fear and cold, they tear your home apart in search of "evidence." Drawers are emptied onto the floor, mattresses cut open, and pictures torn from their frames. Nothing is sacred. During one arrest, NKVD snoopers found a tiny coffin with a child's body awaiting burial. They dumped the body onto the floor and then searched the coffin. Sick people were tossed out of bed and their bandages unwound in case anything should be hidden beneath them.

When they've finished, they clap on the handcuffs and push you out the door. No time for goodbyes. The best you can manage is a quick look into the watery eyes of your wife and a wince at the whimperings of your children. The hallway is empty; for although your neighbors were awakened by the commotion, they are too scared to peer out. They are thinking of themselves and their families. They know what is happening and that there is nothing they can do to help. Fear has big eyes.

A "Black Maria" waits at curbside. This black police truck is like a large American moving van with a row of air holes near the top. Each night fleets of Black Marias sped through Soviet cities with their cargoes of the doomed.

Prisoners were unloaded at local NKVD headquarters, which was usually attached to a prison. The most dreaded prison, the Lubyanka, is near Moscow's central tourist area, famous for its hotels and such theaters as the Bolshoi. Its name inspired such terror that people walked blocks out of their way to avoid passing in front of it. The Lubyanka's evil reputation was (and still is) well deserved. It was very quiet inside, except for the screams echoing through the corridors at night. Newcomers were locked in "dog-kennels," tiny solitary-confinement cells. Sometimes the peephole in the door was surrounded by a painted, glaring eye; other cells were painted blood-red. Solitary confinement was the first step in breaking a prisoner's resistance.

After a few days in solitary confinement, the prisoner was brought to an examiner's office. Neither had any privacy. The prisoner faced the examiner across a desk; the examiner faced a large picture of Stalin hung on the wall opposite, watching his every action. Politely he asked the prisoner to confess and name his accomplices. The examiner didn't mention what crime he was accused of, only that he had to confess. It was up to him to describe his crime—quickly. Stalin demanded confessions from all prisoners, even the most humble. Confessions gave the color of legality to his tyranny and proved that plots existed, as charged in the Moscow Show Trials.

If the prisoner refused to confess, stronger methods were used. At first the NKVD put prisoners on the "conveyor." For days at a time, prisoners were kept awake and questioned by a series of examiners, replaced every few hours as if on a conveyor belt. After two or three days without sleep, one begins to see things. People's faces shimmer. Flies buzz inside his head. Smoke rises before his eyes, which he must keep open; closing them brought a kick in the shins or a slap in the face. The conveyor broke nearly everyone within a week. Its only problem was that Stalin thought a week was too long.

Stalin ordered a speedup. Examiners, he said, must beat prisoners without mercy until they got confessions. Since ordinary citizens weren't put on trial, their appearance didn't matter.

The NKVD made a science of torture. Eighteen-year-old NKVD recruits were taken to torture chambers in the Lubyanka and elsewhere, just as medical students visit hospital wards to learn from expert doctors. They saw prisoners beaten with chair legs, clubs, and rubber hoses. Men were smashed in the stomach with sandbags until they passed out, were revived, and smashed again. For variety, salt water was poured into a victim until he reached the bursting point. Others were put into boxes swarming with bedbugs or had their teeth drilled with dentist's tools. Prisoners' wives and children were beaten before their eyes; some died, or were crippled, or went insane. This was all the more terrible since the last tsars had made it illegal to touch, much less torture, anyone accused of a crime. No civilized ruler harmed suspects' families. But here again Stalin played by his own rules.

Nearly everyone confessed, and the few who didn't were simply shot. People said anything to end their sufferings. A group of peasants admitted to putting a spell on Stalin. One man said he'd planned to throw stones into Kronstadt harbor so as to cripple the Soviet fleet. Another explained his idea of building several artificial volcanoes to explode the entire Soviet Union. Even children confessed to treason. After hard questioning, 160 youngsters aged twelve to fourteen admitted to spying for the Gestapo. One ten-year-old broke down and confessed to acts of treason going back three years; that is, to the time when he was *seven!*

Meanwhile, prisoners' families went through their own tortures. Wives were not told where their husbands had been taken. To find out, they had to go from prison to prison, begging for information. Lines outside prison information offices were long and moved slowly. In Leningrad, women waited five days and nights to ask a clerk the all-important question. If lucky, they learned their husband was inside. If not, they might wander for weeks before learning his whereabouts. Many never learned; their men vanished and were never heard from again.

Belonging to the family of an "enemy of the people" was like having a contagious disease. Friends and relatives would have nothing to do with them; neighbors turned their backs. Working wives lost their jobs and had to get by as best they could. Often they sold possessions to put food on the table. Some sold their bodies, resorting to prostitution.

Life was hardest on the children, especially those who'd lost both parents. Homeless, with no one to turn to for help, they became desperate. Desperation led four teenagers to steal a pistol and commit suicide in a forest outside Moscow. The daughter of Alexander Karin, a high-ranking Red Army officer, was thirteen when her parents were shot. Yezhov's men threw her into the street. She went to her father's best friend, a kindly man who put her up for the night but sent her away in the morning to protect his own family. She returned two months later, pale, thin, her eyes filled with bitterness. No one, she cried, cared if she lived or died. Everyone was against her. At a meeting of the Young Pioneers, she had to damn her parents as spies and give thanks for their execution. All this while, Soviet newspapers praised Stalin's "touching love for children."

The purge spread through society like an oil slick. Life in the Soviet Union became a nightmare of fear and uncertainty. No one knew what to expect from day to day. Trust between people no longer existed. When you left home, you put on your "Soviet street face," a blank expression that gave no hint of your thoughts; only fools showed their feelings in streets swarming with informers. People grew quiet, timid, with their best friends. Things became so bad, said the writer Isaak Babel, that "today a man only talks freely with his wife—at night, with the blankets pulled over his head." A dark cloud of fear hovered over the U.S.S.R., and its name was Joseph Stalin. Brave generals cringed in his presence; his officials were said to wet their pants when he entered a room.

When Stalin felt that the people were completely terrorized, he brought the purge to an end. In the autumn of 1938 Yezhov was transferred from the NKVD to the Water Transportation department. Lavrenty P. Beria, a pale, plump little man with soft, sweaty hands, took his place. Beria was a man after Stalin's heart, sneaky, vicious, deadly; he'd serve Stalin for the rest of

The chiefs of terror. NKVD chief Genrikh Yagoda, who oversaw the Great Purge, before falling victim to it. Below, Lavrenty Beria, whose appointment to head the NKVD marked the end of the Purge. He would hold his position until Stalin's death.

his life. Beria proved his loyalty by sentencing his eighty-year-old stepfather to ten years' hard labor in a prison camp.

Yezhov disappeared. Stalin later told an aide: "Yezhov was a rat; he killed many innocent people. We shot him for that." Apparently the aide, who knew where Yezhov's orders came from, kept a straight face. The Great Purge was over.

Between seven and nine million people were purged between 1936 and 1938. Of these, close to a million were shot. The remainder went to lingering deaths in the *gulag*.

The word *"gulag"* is an acronym of the Russian for Chief Administration for Corrective Labor Camps. It is the Communist version of the old system of forced labor, only more terrible than anything known under the tsars.

As we've seen, the tsars exiled common criminals and revolutionaries to Siberia. While revolutionaries were isolated in remote settlements where they might do as they pleased, even have their familes with them, criminals were put to forced labor. Many died of overwork and harsh treatment, but the object was still to punish, not to kill them. When they'd served their term, they were released. The number at forced labor was never more than 32,000 at any given time; the total of all such prisoners in tsarist times was under 184,000.

When the Russian Revolution began, the Provisional Government abolished exile and forced labor as unworthy of a free people. All political prisoners, including Stalin, were released as soon as Tsar Nicholas II gave up his throne.

The *gulag* came into being almost from the moment the Bolsheviks seized power. In January 1918 Lenin ordered the first corrective labor camps set up. Their aim, he declared, was "purging the Russian land of all kinds of harmful insects." By "insects" he meant anyone who opposed his Revolution or who could not be trusted. They were to be punished by "forced labor of the hardest kind." In fact, they became slaves condemned to toil under inhuman conditions and without hope of freedom. The Soviet Union now became the only major country in the twentieth century to have a permanent slave labor system.

The system begun by Lenin was expanded many times over by Stalin. Swarms of humanity passed through the *gulag* as Stalin's power increased. During the 1920s, tens of thousands of Trotskyites, former members of non-Communist political parties, and religious believers formed the bulk of the *gulag* population. In the next decade there came hundreds of thousands of "wreckers" and others sacrificed to the Five-Year Plans. Kulaks and peasants, followed by victims of the purge, came by the millions in the middle and late thirties. The Second World War added millions more "enemies of the people."

Although the number of camps in the *gulag* was a state secret, it is believed that Stalin had 125 camps and camp clusters, major camps each with dozens of branches. These camps, together with their surrounding lands, equaled an area larger than any European country. Their population varied from year to year. As near as we can tell, in 1938 the *gulag* held eight million slaves, mostly victims of the purge. Its population never fell below this figure, and may have climbed to fifteen million after the Second World War—a population as large as Czechoslovakia's, or that of Belgium and Austria combined, in the 1940s. No country in history ever had so many slaves as the Workers' Paradise. When Abraham Lincoln issued the Emancipation Proclamation in 1862, there were fewer than four million slaves in the United States.

The NKVD was not only Stalin's secret police, but, as rulers of the *gulag*, a gigantic, murdering, slave empire run for profit. There were few industries in which the NKVD didn't have a share. In addition to the camps, it had divisions for building roads, railroads, canals, bridges, and tunnels. NKVD factories produced much of the nation's bricks, cement, tractors, steamrollers, farming equipment, furniture, shoes, and underwear. Half the U.S.S.R.'s lumber came from NKVD forests and sawmills.

Certain key projects were completely in NKVD hands. The Baltic–White Sea Canal was built by 250,000 slaves working under its whips. There were even special *gulag* prisons for scientists. These people, all of whom were supposedly traitors, worked on top-secret projects. The best equipment and the latest scientific journals were made available to them. Some made real contributions to the Soviet military. Experts in aviation, explosives, artillery, and electronics designed new weapons. In the 1950s, hundreds of captive scientists, mathematicians, and engineers did atomic research; when they finished their work and were no longer needed, they were sent to hard labor because they knew too much about the Soviet atomic bomb. Professor Korolev, future father of the Soviet space program, spent years in Moscow's Special Prison Number 4.

Control of the *gulag* made the NKVD the nation's largest employer. At least one Soviet worker in five—some experts say one in four—was a slave. Unlike other countries, whose slaves were cared for as valuable property, the goal of Soviet slavery was to destroy enemies while profiting from their labor. Lenin and Stalin thought it wasteful to kill enemies outright unless absolutely necessary. Their enemies were under sentence of death, but it was postponed for a few months or years. Fed little and worked hard, they added their mite to Soviet power before dying.

Stalin boasted that the U.S.S.R. was the only country without unemployment. He was right, but he never told the whole story. His slaves died so quickly that replacements were always in demand for the *gulag*. Work on the Baltic–White Sea

Canal, for example, killed 700 people a day. But with 1,500 new prisoners arriving daily, the number working on the project actually increased. Total deaths in the *gulag* during the Stalin years were at least twelve million men and women.

Most of Stalin's slave labor camps were located in two areas. One was the basin of the Pechora River of northwestern Russia near the Arctic Circle, an area larger than New York, New Jersey, and New England combined. This is tundra, a vast treeless plain lashed by ferocious winds blowing from the North Pole. Although the topsoil thaws in summer, creating shallow swamps infested by mosquitoes, the warmth never reaches the permafrost, subsoil permanently frozen solid to a depth of a thousand feet. South of the tundra is the taiga, a forest belt of spruce and fir stretching eastward, clear across Siberia.

The NKVD had scores of camps in the Pechora Basin, along the rail line from Kotlas to Vorkuta. Over a million men and women worked here at any given time, mining coal, drilling for oil, and lumbering. Lumbering was the real killer. Men were forced to work in temperatures of −40° Fahrenheit. Under the watchful eyes of their guards, they stood in waist-deep snow, cutting trees all day. Scarcely a day passed without somebody being crushed by one of the falling giants. Since there were no horses or tractors to haul the logs to the sawmills, men harnessed themselves to the logs and dragged them across snowfields. A prisoner who escaped described life for Stalin's lumberjacks:

> The prisoners were called at two o'clock in the morning to get up. At three o'clock they were started off to their work of sawing, stacking, etc., the lumber. Each prisoner had a certain job to do each day before he was allowed to go back to the barracks and get something to eat. . . . Those who were not able to finish their

job by eleven o'clock [in the evening] . . . got nothing
whatever to eat. They were made to stay in the woods
until they did finish their job and then go right on to
the next day's job without food or sleep as punishment. . . . The work is so strenuous that many of the
laborers die every day. Women have to do the same
hard work.

The other group of camps was in Siberia, more than 1,500
miles beyond the settlements Stalin knew as a young man.
Many of these camps were located in the basin of the Kolyma
River, which empties into the East Siberian Sea, an arm of
the Arctic Ocean. The Kolyma is icebound nine months of
the year, and for two months the sun doesn't rise at all. The
land is wind-blasted, bleak and desolate. Here in Oymyakon,
the coldest town on earth, temperatures plunge to $-96°$ Fahrenheit. It is so cold that one's nostrils become clogged with
ice and every breath causes stinging in the chest. Stalin's slaves
called Kolyma the "wonderful planet":

> *Kolyma, Kolyma*
> *Wonderful planet*
> *Twelve months winter,*
> *The rest summer.*

They also called it the Land of White Death. Kolyma was hell
frozen over.

Gold brought the Russians to Kolyma. The area was first
mapped and tested for mineral wealth in the 1920s. Mining
began in the early thirties, just when Stalin needed large sums
of money for his Five-Year Plans. Since the climate was so
harsh, and he wanted the mines to be as profitable as possible,
he decided to use slaves on a scale unheard of even in Soviet
Russia. Their story is one of the saddest ever recorded.

The prisoners' ordeal began with a train ride. They were packed into cattle cars for the first leg of the journey to Siberia. The cattle cars were unheated in winter; once an entire train-load, more than a thousand prisoners and guards, froze to death. In summer, the cars' roofs glowed under the sun's rays, sending up shimmering heat waves. It was so crowded that prisoners ate standing up, slept standing up, and died standing up. The dead were not even noticed, held up by the bodies of the living, until the train halted for an hour or two every few days. There were no toilets, and the prisoners sometimes stood ankle-deep in filth.

After seven weeks, they reached Vladivostok on the Sea of Japan. Here began a Middle Passage like that of the blacks brought from Africa to the New World. The only difference was that the blacks were crowded into hot, stuffy holds, while Stalin's slaves braved the cold. The ships' holds contained a series of iron cages and the guards had machine guns. But their main weapon against rebellion were fire hoses able to flood the cages with icy seawater.

Some ships made unscheduled stops before arriving at their destination, the port of Magadan, entryway to the Kolyma territory. If a ship sailed too late in autumn, it might be trapped in pack ice far from land, as happened to the *Dzhurma* in 1933. Next spring, when she broke free, not one of her 12,000 prisoners remained alive.

Arrival at Magadan even after a normal voyage was heart-breaking. As soon as the ship docked, guards with rifles and fixed bayonets hustled the prisoners ashore. The dead were laid out on the stony beach and counted, for the *gulag*'s masters kept accurate records. The living were addressed by an officer. "I must tell you," said a major Vostokov, "that you are not brought here to live but to suffer and die. If you live . . . it means that you are guilty of one of two things: either you worked less than was assigned you or you ate more than your proper due." After that, prisoners went to the slave market, where the commanders of various mining camps looked them over. The commanders felt their muscles and opened their mouths to check their teeth. From Magadan they were sent to camp on foot or by steamboat if the Kolyma was free of ice.

Camp was not a welcome sight for Stalin's slaves. From the distance they saw a large enclosure ringed by barbed-wire fences topped with coils of razor wire, thousands of two-inch razor blades joined together. The fences were reinforced every thirty yards by watchtowers crowned by machine gun nests. Marching through the main gate, the prisoners saw the camp motto overhead, such as "In the Soviet Union Labor is a Matter of Honor, Prowess, and Heroism" or "Long Live Great Stalin."

Once inside, prisoners were assigned to huts, large unpainted wooden boxes with oiled paper instead of glass for window panes. The first thing they noticed upon entering was the stench. It wasn't merely unpleasant. It was an overpowering smell that assaulted the nostrils with a mixture of filth, sweat, decay, dirty rags, and unwashed feet. Inmates slept not in beds, but in bunks on mattresses filled with hard-packed sawdust. They slept five to a bunk, close together to share body warmth. Disease and parasites were also shared. The bunks crawled with bedbugs, which tormented their victims, preventing them from getting a full night's sleep. Outside, searchlights crisscrossed over the enclosure, probing every corner. Guards patrolled with wolfhounds, great gray beasts that could track down an escapee and tear him to pieces.

Wake-up in Kolyma was 5:00 A.M. in summer, 5:30 A.M. in winter. An iron rail dangling from a chain was beaten with a crowbar, jarring the prisoners awake. Guards ran through the huts, pulling raggedy blankets off bunks and shouting, "Come on, come on, get up, faster, faster!" Dressing quickly, they stumbled out to the parade ground. Clothes were cotton pants and jackets, patched and flimsy, tied around with bits of string; faces were wound in rags to prevent frostbite. Feet were wrapped in odd pieces of cloth instead of socks, stuffed into shoes made of birch bark or old rubber tires.

A medical orderly now appeared for sick call. A harsh man, his object was not to excuse people, but to send as many as possible to the work site. "I am sick," says a man with hollow cheeks and sunken eyes. The orderly feels his pulse and says he's all right. Then a guard hits him with a rubber hose and kicks him outside, where it is −40° Fahrenheit. "I am sick," says a naked man burning with fever. The orderly feels his pulse and says that he, too, must work. The guard flings him headfirst through the door, tossing his clothes after him. He must dress within minutes or freeze to death.

Outside, the men have finished their breakfast of stale bread and putrid fish heads and are forming work details on the parade ground. This is an important time for the guards, who must account for everyone before opening the gate. The prisoners are counted and recounted. The guards had better get things right, for their necks are on the line. Stalin had ruled that if a prisoner escapes, his guards must take his place. Everyone is present and the gate swings open.

Men at Kolyma did twelve to sixteen hours of hard physical labor each day, every day, except for the occasional day off every few months. Refusal to work was punished in various ways. In some camps refusers were shot instantly. In others they were sent to "isolators" or "Stalin villas." Ex-prisoner Aleksandr I. Solzhenitsyn described these hellholes in his book *One Day in the Life of Ivan Denisovich*:

> The fellows from [hut] 104 had built the place themselves and knew how it looked—stone walls, a concrete floor, and no window. There was a stove, but that was

only enough to melt the ice on the walls and make puddles on the floor. You slept on bare boards and your teeth chattered all night. You got six ounces of bread a day and they only gave you hot gruel every third day.

Ten days! If you had ten days in the cells here and sat them out to the end, it meant you'd be a wreck for the rest of your life. You got TB [tuberculosis] and you'd never be out of hospitals as long as you lived.

And the fellows who did fifteen days were dead and buried.

Stalin treated animals better than humans. Horses not only ate better, they had private stalls and warm blankets. A guard dog's ration was twice that of a prisoner's. And the prisoner had to earn that food. Everyone had to do a set daily amount of work, regardless of strength or ability, to receive a normal ration, barely enough to keep one alive. Doing more work brought slightly more food; doing less meant having less food. You couldn't win. A man who worked hard to fill his belly might die of a heart attack from overwork. In time even the strongest tired, did less, and had his rations cut. Now began a vicious circle. Undernourishment made him less able to meet his quota, which meant less and less food until his energy gave out. He became a "goner." Goners were put on a starvation diet and forced to do lighter work until they died. Camp commanders with too many goners shot them; in one camp they were herded into a minefield and blown to bits.

Life in the *gulag* was an unbroken round of cold, filth, hunger, and terror. There were always public executions for the slightest infraction of the rules. Complaints about the food were "counterrevolutionary agitation," as was keeping silent while prisoners shouted "Long live Stalin!" Both offenses brought a bullet in the neck. Entire work details were shot for failure to produce enough gold. There were also special extermination camps where slaves were killed in large numbers. A radio message might come to a gold-mining camp from Moscow: "Liquidate five hundred enemies of the people." If names were given, the victims had to step forward; if not, anyone might be chosen at random. Their arms were bound with wire, they were tossed into a truck, and driven to the extermination camp to be shot.

Women suffered as well as men in Kolyma. Although they weren't sent to the gold mines, they chopped wood and worked as fish-packers in Magadan. There are touching stories of meetings between groups of men and women slaves, who almost never saw one another:

> Then the men notice the women for the first time. Both sexes flock to the wire. The men and women shouted and stretched out their hands to each other; almost all were weeping openly. "You poor loves, you darlings! Cheer up! Be brave! Be strong!" arose from both sides of the wire. Then they threw each other presents across the wire—torn towels, saucepans made out of stolen prison mugs, even bread.

The Land of White Death claimed a quarter of those who died in the *gulag*. No fewer than three million people died there during the Stalin years. In human terms, this meant that each kilogram of Kolyma gold cost one life, a ton of gold a thousand lives.

Kolyma was Stalin's version of Auschwitz, Hitler's huge camp for killing Jews in Poland during the Second World War. Hitler, when criticized for his death camps, once cried, "If I had the vast spaces of Siberia, I wouldn't need concentration camps." The Nazi *Fuehrer* (Leader) knew that he and Stalin were two of a kind—killers. And he admired that quality in his fellow tyrant.

THE PACT OF BLOOD

LENIN LIKED TO CALL MOSCOW "THE GENERAL HEADQUARTERS of the World Revolution." This reveals a lot about the Bolshevik leaders and their view of the outside world. They were Marxists, people with a mission. Not content with seizing power in their own country, they meant to spread communism worldwide. There could be no other way, since, they believed, capitalism and communism could never live in peace. One had to perish so the other might live.

Soon after the Bolshevik Revolution, Lenin decided that the U.S.S.R. must deal with other nations in two ways. It must have normal trade and diplomatic relations to enable it to develop in peace. And at the same time, it must secretly undermine foreign governments, clearing the way for Communist revolution. Thus, for the first time in history a great nation became the center of a conspiracy to overthrow every other government in the name of an idea.

The chief weapon in this secret war was the Comintern, or Communist International, created by Lenin in 1919. The Comintern grew out of his idea of the Communist Party as a select group of disciplined fighters taking orders from a high command. The Comintern was to help Marxist revolutionaries form Communist parties in every nation. When Communist parties joined the Comintern, they promised "to render every possible assistance to the Soviet Republics in their struggle" against non-Communist states. Thus their true loyalty was not to their own country, but to the U.S.S.R.; indeed, they had to betray their country, even fight against it, on Moscow's orders.

146

Member parties were to act legally, taking part in political campaigns and electing candidates to public office. But just as most of an iceberg is invisible underwater, most Comintern activities were to be underground and illegal. From the beginning, the Comintern set out to break the law in foreign countries. Here again the end justified the means. Anything was moral, Lenin believed, if it helped the World Revolution.

The Comintern had several departments to handle its underground work, all controlled, funded, and manned by the Soviet secret police. A forgery department copied passports and identity papers, vital if agents were to enter a country illegally and blend in with its population. A terror department handled "wet jobs," assassinations in foreign countries. The intelligence department recruited spies and handled information gathering. Through the years the Comintern gathered the names of thousands of people willing to betray their countries at Moscow's command. Some were simple workers, other important scientists who'd pass secrets to Moscow. In addition, every Soviet citizen traveling abroad became a Comintern spy, receiving a thorough grilling about what they'd seen as soon as they returned home. Reporters for Tass, the official news agency, often doubled as spies.

The Comintern's first tests came immediately after the First World War. In the spring of 1919, Comintern agents helped local Communists seize power in Hungary. They began a reign of terror that ended only when government supporters rallied to crush the rebellion. Asia, too, felt the Comintern's influence. In June 1921, its agents brought together a few Chinese students of Marxism. At a meeting in a girl's school in Shanghai, China's largest city, they founded the Chinese Communist Party. Among its leaders was a young library assistant named Mao Tse-tung. In the years to come, Mao would lead the revolution that created the People's Republic of China.

But from the beginning the Comintern's chief target was

Germany, the land of Karl Marx and, Lenin felt, the key to
Europe. Early in 1919, Comintern agents helped form the
German Communist Party. Soon afterward, Communist-led
revolutions exploded in Germany's major cities. "Red Guards"
built barricades in the capital, Berlin. Rebels set up a "Soviet
republic" in Munich and began a German version of the Red
Terror. Communist troops went on a rampage of looting and
burning; anyone who opposed them, or anyone they disliked
for any reason, was murdered.

The Weimar Republic, the democratic government that
replaced the German Empire at the end of the war, had to
fight for its life. Since the Allies had forced Germany to disband
nearly its entire army, the republic's leaders called for volunteers to fight the Reds. Volunteers came in the thousands,
veterans of the trenches hardened by countless battles on the
Western Front. They formed bands, or Free Corps, with such
names as the Iron Division and Viking League.

The revolutionaries met fighters as bloodthirsty as themselves. Free Corpsmen hated Communists, considering them
traitors. Now they took their revenge—and what revenge! Free
Corps units stormed the Reds' strongholds. Prisoners, as well
as innocent bystanders, were massacred wholesale. Bodies lay
so thick in the gutters of downtown Munich that it was hard
to pass without stepping into pools of blood.

The Weimar Republic survived and began to gain popular
support. Among its chief supporters was the Social Democratic
Party, Marxists committed to democracy and unwilling to become Moscow's puppets. Unlike Bolsheviks, Social Democrats
trusted ordinary people to control their lives. They believed
in real trade unions that could strike and participate in free
elections. Social Democrats supported the republic because it
allowed them to achieve their aims peacefully.

Communist revolution had been crushed in Germany, but

not the Communists. During the 1920s, the German Communist Party grew as unemployment increased. When Stalin became dictator, he vowed to destroy the Weimar Republic and bring Germany under Communist control. He ordered the Comintern and German Communists to undermine the republic by attacking its supporters. A vicious campaign was launched against the Social Democrats. Communist propaganda branded them "fools," "traitors to the working class," and "agents of capitalism." Words quickly escalated into violence as both parties formed their own armies and began to fight pitched battles in the streets. Roving gangs broke up opponents' meetings with clubs, knives, and brass knuckles; there were even gunfights. The police often found it impossible to control the violence.

Things grew worse when a new force, the Nazis, came on the scene. The Nazis—National Socialist German Workers' Party—were founded in Munich in 1920 by Adolf Hitler. Hitler, born in Austria in 1889, had served bravely as a soldier in World War I and was a cunning politician. He was also a man filled with hate. Most of all, he hated Jews, who he felt were an inferior race and the cause of all the evil in the world. Democracy was a "Jewish invention" meant to give power to the weak and ignorant. Communism was a "Jewish plot"; after all, Trotsky, Zinoviev, Kamenev, and other Bolshevik leaders were Jews, as was Marx himself, although they'd abandoned their religion for atheism.

But although Hitler hated "Jewish-Marxism," he admired the Bolsheviks. They, like his Nazis, were fanatics who thought nothing of mass murder. He read the writings of Lenin and Trotsky and was an avid student of Soviet terror methods. When he came to power, he modeled his Gestapo—Secret State Police—on the NKVD.

Hitler turned Soviet terror methods against his enemies,

especially the German Communists. He formed his most devoted followers into a private army called the storm troopers. Mostly war veterans and ex-Free Corps fighters, the storm troopers dressed in brown uniforms and marched under the swastika flag, a twisted cross against a red background; Hitler had taken the red background from the Communists' own banners. As they marched, Hitler's bully-boys sang savage songs:

> *The red rats, the red rats,*
> *Up against the wall with the red rats.*

The Communists took the challenge and, by the early 1930s, hundreds from both sides were dying each year in street clashes.

Stalin welcomed the Nazis' growing power; in 1930, its candidates for the *Reichstag*, Germany's parliament, won 6.5 million votes. Their good showing, he said, proved that the German people were growing tired of democracy.

The next year, Stalin made an important decision. His German puppets were ordered to step up attacks on the Social Democrats even if that meant helping the Nazis. Since he hated democracy, any gain for its enemies must also be a gain for Communism, he thought.

Strange things began to happen as a result of Stalin's decision. Communist and Nazi thugs might slaughter each other in brawls, but their Reichstag representatives voted together against the republic and its supporters. Communists and Nazis staged paralyzing strikes and joined forces on the picket lines, each wearing the uniform of his party's army. Strangest of all, hammer-and-sickle flags hung beside swastika banners in workers' neighborhoods.

The fact that Stalin was helping Communism's sworn enemy seems not to have troubled him at all. For in the words of a Communist slogan, "After Hitler, our turn." Stalin, the Greatest Genius of All Times and Peoples, knew that Nazi rule wouldn't last long. Hitler would make such a mess of things that the Germans would toss him out and turn to the German Communist Party.

Hitler became chancellor—head of the German government—in January 1933, thanks in part to Communist help. Stalin had made a stupid, monstrous blunder. That blunder, the first of several concerning Hitler, would cost millions of Russian lives.

"Heads will roll!" was one of Hitler's favorite expressions. That was a promise, not a threat. Like Stalin, he set out to destroy anyone who stood in his way. He declared the Nazis Germany's only political party, and smashed all the others. Their headquarters were raided and their leaders arrested, together with thousands of rank-and-file members. Prisoners were sent to a field outside the sleepy village of Dachau, where barracks surrounded by barbed wire had been hastily built. Dachau was Hitler's first concentration camp, his own type of *gulag*. Whether they liked each other's company or not, German Communists and Social Democrats were together at last.

Hitler ended unemployment by spending billions of marks to rebuild Germany's military strength. Once again factories hummed with activity as the latest types of weapons rolled off assembly lines. Here, too, he learned from the Soviets. German officers knew about Marshal Tukhachevsky's experiments with paratroops. At a time when others had doubts about dropping soldiers from airplanes, they copied the Soviets in forming airborne divisions. Within a few years, the Nazi Fuehrer had the deadliest war machine the world had ever seen. And he meant to use it.

Hitler made no secret of his intention to stamp out "Jewish-Marxism." He discussed it in his book, *Mein Kampf—My Struggle*—and in speeches over a ten-year period. In 1936 and

1937, he persuaded Japan and Italy to join Germany in an Anti-Comintern Pact. Although they pledged to fight together against Communism, the Pact masked their plans to attack smaller, weaker nations.

Stalin became frightened. The Red Army, he knew, was no match for the Nazi war machine. Though larger in numbers, its troops were poorly trained and led, especially after the purge took its toll. His only hope was to find allies. And those allies could only be the hated democracies: Great Britain, France, and the United States.

The Comintern was ordered to stop denouncing the democracies. Instead, it was to help form "Popular Fronts" to weld Hitler's enemies into an alliance. Suddenly local Communist parties, guided by the Comintern, pretended to be patriots and called for a war to save democracy. In the United States, the American Communist Party no longer called for revolution and a "Soviet Socialist America." Communists claimed to be true followers of Thomas Jefferson and Abraham Lincoln. "Communism," said the *Daily Worker*, the Party newspaper in the U.S., "is twentieth-century Americanism." The U.S.S.R., too, was a "democracy," although nobody explained how that fit in with faked trials and *gulag* slavery.

In many countries, Communists set up "front" organizations. These were clubs, committees, and foundations dedicated to some worthy cause but actually tools of the Comintern. For example, Communists, who usually kept their Party membership secret, might set up a discussion group on world peace at a university. The group would attract students and teachers interested in the subject. Properly guided, the group would then demonstrate in favor of Stalin's policies. Those in the know called such groups "Innocents' Clubs," because their members didn't realize how they were being used.

Communists were also skilled at worming their way into

labor unions. The idea was to fight for workers' rights while quietly taking over the union. Once in control, the Communists could make propaganda, instigate strikes, or carry out sabotage under Moscow's direction. Sometimes, however, Communists demanded reforms such as social security that were later adopted by governments.

In France and Spain, Communists joined other parties to form Popular Front governments, which soon proved to be failures. The French Popular Front government collapsed when the Communist Party quarreled with its partners. The Spanish Popular Front government became involved in a bloody civil war.

In July 1936, a group of generals revolted, claiming the government was leading Spain to ruin. The Spanish Civil War quickly drew in foreign powers. General Francisco Franco, commander of the rebel forces, appealed to Hitler and Italian dictator Benito Mussolini for help. They gave generously; planes, tanks, even entire army divisions, were sent to fight alongside Franco's troops.

The Spanish government, too, appealed for help. But the democracies, fearing a wider war, declared their neutrality. Only Stalin was willing to help. The U.S.S.R. sent weapons and supplies to the Spanish government, but demanded a high price for its services. In return for weapons, Spain had to send its gold reserves to Moscow for safekeeping; the gold is still there. Moreover, Stalin demanded control of Spain's armed forces and, increasingly, of its government. The NKVD took over the police forces in many cities and began hunting down "enemies of the people." Socialists, union leaders, and those who disagreed with the Communists were shot. Spain's ordeal continued until Franco destroyed the republic and made himself dictator in 1939, imposing a new ordeal upon the nation.

Stalin had hoped that support for Spain would encourage

the democracies to join him against Hitler. But Great Britain and France were suspicious. Their governments knew that leopards don't change their spots. Besides, their military staffs had followed the purge carefully. They knew that the Red Army high command had been slaughtered and that an army without good leaders was like a brainless giant. There was also something they didn't know. At the very moment Stalin was calling for an alliance against Hitler, he was secretly trying to become his friend.

Hitler had always demanded *Lebensraum,* living space in the east for Germany's growing population. Already he'd taken over Austria and Czechoslovakia through bullying and threats of war. By 1939, he was ready for his next victim: Poland. This time, however, he expected resistance. Great Britain, France, and the U.S.S.R. each had defense treaties with Poland. If he attacked, and they honored their treaties, he'd have to fight on two fronts, an idea that sent chills up his spine. Somehow he had to keep the U.S.S.R. out of the war, perhaps even make it an ally.

Stalin believed he could turn Hitler's problem to his own advantage. By offering Hitler his friendship, he'd guarantee a war between Germany and the democracies. Hitler would attack and conquer Poland easily, only to face a bigger war in the west. Stalin wanted that war, which he expected to be a replay of the First World War. It would drag on for years, exhausting both sides while the U.S.S.R. grew stronger. Then Stalin's moment would come. His armies would roll westward, unstoppable, conquering Europe from Poland to Portugal.

Stalin quietly hinted that the U.S.S.R. and Germany needn't be enemies. Both hated the democracies and that hatred should bind them together. Hitler took the hint and sent diplomats to work out a treaty. In the Treaty of Non-Aggression both sides promised to be friends and remain neutral if the other went to war. A secret section also settled the boundaries of Eastern Europe. In the event of war with Poland, Germany would have the western part of the country; Russia could take eastern Poland and do as she pleased with the Baltic nations— Estonia, Latvia, Lithuania, Finland—without German interference. The Anti-Comintern Pact was conveniently forgotten. "The Pact of Blood," as the treaty would soon be called, was signed on August 23, 1939.

That night Stalin entertained his new friends in the Kremlin. Champagne flowed, and soon everyone was drunk. Nazis and Communists grinned, shook hands, and hugged one another warmly. It was like a gangster convention; they'd fought, and might fight again, but they were in the same business: tyranny and murder. Stalin had only kind words for the man he'd once called a "beast." "I know how much the German nation loves its Fuehrer," he said, drinking a toast to Hitler's health. "The Soviet government takes the new pact very seriously. I can guarantee on my word of honor that the Soviet Union will not betray its partner."

We don't know what Hitler thought of Stalin's "word of honor." But when he heard that the treaty was signed, he went wild with joy. "*Now I have the world in my pocket!*" he shouted. With a stroke of the pen, the dictators had doomed Poland and triggered the Second World War.

At 4:00 A.M., September 1, 1940, Hitler unleashed his *Blitzkrieg* ("lightning war") against Poland. Without bothering to declare war, swarms of planes with swastika markings streaked eastward with their cargoes of death. Soon flames from Polish airfields, oil depots, and ammunition dumps were leaping skyward to create a false dawn. As the sun rose, tank divisions followed by masses of infantry surged forward. The Poles fought

Stalin and German Foreign Minister von Ribbentrop smile after completing the Treaty of Non-Aggression on August 23, 1939.

bravely, but they never had a chance. The Nazis blasted through one defense line after another, driving the Poles before them. Although Great Britain and France declared war on Germany, they could do little for their ally without Soviet support.

Stalin supported Hitler. On September 17, as a shocked world looked on, Marshal Semyon Konstantinovich Timoshenko led the Red Army into eastern Poland. That was the deathblow. Soviets and Germans met at Brest-Litovsk, where twenty-one years earlier the Bolsheviks had been forced to sign a humiliating peace treaty. This time they turned their guns on a common enemy. When the city surrendered, they held a joint victory parade with hammer-and-sickle and swastika flags waving side by side.

The victors now began to destroy the Polish nation. Western Poland was put under a Nazi governor backed by troops and the Gestapo. They began to "clean house." Thousands of Polish noblemen, priests, teachers, lawyers, doctors, journalists—all who might lead or offer resistance—were shot. All Jews were marked for death. Special Action Groups, a polite name for murder squads, fanned out over the countryside. Hundreds of Jews at a time were marched into forests in midwinter. Despite bitter cold, they were forced to strip naked and stand at the edge of a deep pit, where machine-gunners mowed them down. Millions of other Jews were herded into sealed-off sections of cities, or "ghettos," to wait their turn with the executioners. There were so many to kill that Hitler later built special "death camps" at Auschwitz and other sites in Poland.

The Soviets were no better than the Nazis; in fact, many Poles thought them worse. Once the fighting stopped, large areas of eastern Poland became part of White Russia and the Ukraine, where they remain today. To make sure things went smoothly, Stalin sent NKVD troops into the occupied areas.

Like their Gestapo allies, the NKVD were ruthless. Arriving in a town a few days after the Red Army, they began making mass arrests of people, including their whole families, who might oppose Soviet rule. Those not shot immediately were held in prisons until locomotives pulling long lines of filthy, stinking cattle cars came chugging into the local railroad station. When a defiant prisoner shouted that there were thirty million Poles, and they'd never let their country be enslaved, an NKVD officer smirked. "What's thirty million?" he said. "We've more than that in our prisons as it is." What Stalin had done to his own people, he wouldn't hesitate to do to foreigners, especially Poles, who'd defeated him in 1921. Cold. Starvation. Brutality. Death. It was the same with the Poles as with the kulaks and the purge victims before them.

Sooner or later the survivors arrived at their destinations, usually collective farms. Soviet books still claim these people were deported to save them from the Nazis. But here is how Danuta G. remembered their "kindness" and her life in Siberia; she was twelve and not very good at punctuation:

> [In Russia] I weeded wheat and vegetables I scorched in the sun all day, and late in the evening I came back home tired. . . . I was still very little, I was not strong enough it couldn't be helped. . . . When I came back home to eat one thin flat pancake and lie down to sleep only to wake up tomorrow morning and go for a whole day in the field on just one flat pancake. They called us the worst names they could, in general we don't have enough words to describe what we went through. Everything that goes on in Russia is based on a lie. . . . the holidays I had in Siberia I will probably never have anything like this. There wasn't even a morsel of bread at home, only misery and poverty looked

into our windows. When I went out to beg sometimes I brought back a morsel of bread, and sometimes not even that. My longing was to put a good morsel of bread in my mouth. When we were riding south we saw people rambling about the stations and black from hunger. . . . We don't really find the words to describe these experiences in Russia. It is impossible either to describe or to tell, only that person can understand it who felt it himself on his own skin. Otherwise no one will understand.

Jews learned to hate the Soviets as much as they hated the Nazis. During the winter of 1939–1940, Jews fled to the unoccupied border zone between the two armies. Behind them were Hitler's butchers, thirsty for blood. In front were Stalin's thugs ready to open fire with machine guns if they tried to cross over. During that terrible winter thousands of Jews slept in the open, trapped between Poland's conquerors. Many died. Others gave up hope and returned to the German zone. The few who crossed into Soviet territory found that they'd jumped from the frying pan into the fire. Things were so bad there that people bribed NKVD border guards to let them "escape" to certain death in Nazi-occupied Poland.

Prisoners of war fared just as badly. When Poland surrendered, some 250,000 soldiers, from privates to generals, fell into Soviet hands. Of these, 12,000 common soldiers were sent to Kolyma, where fewer than 600 survived their first year in the mines; the others worked elsewhere in the *gulag*.

Marshal Timoshenko's aide, Nikita Khrushchev, promised that Polish officers would be freed to return home. That promise was never meant to be kept. About 15,000 officers, the cream of the Polish army, were held in three prison camps in western Russia. In April 1940, the prisoners in one camp heard a speech from the camp's NKVD commander. "You are going home," he said, smiling, "to the west." The men cheered, especially when an NKVD band played cheerful farewell tunes. Perhaps some didn't cheer. Perhaps they remembered that "going west" is army slang for being killed.

Several hundred officers were put aboard trains and, sure enough, taken west, to the Katyn Forest ten miles west of Smolensk on the main road to Moscow. There their hands were tied behind their backs and they were marched away in small batches. After a few minutes they stood before a huge pit with mounds of fresh earth on either side. It was the end of the road. Each was grabbed by two NKVD men while a third put a pistol to the back of his neck. He pulled the trigger, sending a bullet upward into the brain until it broke through the forehead. Shootings continued during the next month until 4,500 men lay twelve deep in the pit. Then it was covered and trees were planted to hide the site. The Katyn Massacre was over. *

No one in the West knows the fate of the prisoners in the other two camps. They vanished without a trace. It is said that 6,000 were taken to the shore of the White Sea, and put aboard barges that were towed away and sunk in the icy waters. Perhaps, but there is no evidence. Another 5,000 were last seen near Kharkov in the Ukraine before they vanished. To this day, Poland's Communist government forbids monuments to the murdered officers.

Within weeks of his victory, Stalin cashed in on the secret section of the Pact of Blood. Estonia, Latvia, and Lithuania

---

* The mass grave at Katyn was discovered by advancing German troops in 1943. Stalin said the Germans had put the bodies there themselves, although all the evidence pointed to an NKVD crime. Once, when asked where the other officers were, he telephoned NKVD chief Beria. "Beria," he said, "says they are a long way away and will take a very long time to get here."

were bullied into signing "friendship" treaties giving Moscow naval bases along the Baltic Sea; the countries were taken over completely and annexed to the U.S.S.R. the following year. But when Stalin turned to Finland, he got more than he bargained for.

A glance at the map explains Stalin's interest in Finland. Leningrad is near the Karelian Isthmus, a narrow strip of land between the Gulf of Finland and Lake Ladoga. The Finnish part of Karelia was only twenty miles from Leningrad, within easy artillery range of the sprawling city. Although Stalin had no fear of a Finnish attack, there was no telling what other, more powerful nations might do in the future. He therefore demanded that Finland exchange its part of Karelia and certain naval bases for worthless Soviet territory in the far north. When the Finns refused, he decided to attack, boasting that the Red Army would easily overrun their small army. Some of his generals said the war would last four days, outdoing Hitler's blitzkrieg in Poland. A Finnish proverb might have made them less arrogant: "Don't boast before you fight; you'll end up without your head."

The war would be between the Finnish David and the Soviet Goliath. The Soviets seemed to have all the advantages. Finland, with its population of 4 million, faced a nation of 190 million. This meant that Stalin could lose hundreds of men in killing one Finn and still have Europe's largest army. The Soviets were also superior in every type of weapon: tanks, artillery, aircraft, and warships.

Yet there were weak spots in the Soviet army that would show up once the fighting began. The Red Army, expecting a quick victory, was unprepared for winter fighting. Troops wore lightweight uniforms without overcoats; their underwear was lighter than that worn by Finns in summertime. That would cost lives, for the Finnish winter is harsh. When temperatures dip to $-30°$ or $-40°$ Fahrenheit, Finland's 60,000 lakes freeze hard as concrete and its forests bow under a mantle of snow. Worse, the Red Army man, though brave, was basically an armed slave. Not allowed to think for himself, he was trained simply to follow orders without question. The slightest offenses brought savage beatings; griping, always the soldier's inalienable right, was punished as treason. "The Russian marches to war with a revolver at his back," said a British officer who'd seen the Red Army in action.

Not that the Finns were prepared for war, either. A peace-loving people, they'd voted to build schools and hospitals, spending as little as possible on weapons. Defense Minister Baron Karl von Mannerheim disagreed with that policy. At seventy-two, Mannerheim was Finland's greatest soldier. He had served in the Russian Imperial Army and, during the Bolshevik Revolution, fought for Finland's independence. He despised Bolsheviks and all they stood for. With such a neighbor, he believed, his country had to be strong. But since Finland was a democracy, he had to accept the people's decision. As a result, Finland had a few light tanks and a hundred antitank guns to protect an 800-mile border with the U.S.S.R.

Finland's first line of defense was the Mannerheim Line, a flimsy network of slit-trenches, barricades, and machine gun nests stretching across the Karelian Isthmus. The real strength of the Mannerheim Line was not its weapons, but those behind them. The Finnish soldier was a free man. With his family and home to the rear, he knew what he was fighting for—and against. Over the years scores of fugitives from the *gulag*, living skeletons with wild eyes, had made their way to safety in Finland. The stories they told convinced the Finns that they'd have none of Stalin's "friendship." They'd fight. They'd fight fiercely, against any odds and regardless of cost for what they loved.

The season was their best ally. Finns got used to winter

early in life. In the countryside, they quickly became good skiers, since there was no other way to get around from October to April. Children learned to survive in the wilderness by playing *suunnistaminen*, or find-your-way-in-the-forest. With only a compass and a list of checkpoints, they had to reach a destination within a set time. They also learned to dress for winter survival, which meant wearing layers of warm clothing rather than one heavy coat. The best way to protect the feet was with several pairs of woolen socks in roomy, flexible boots. Soldiers had knee-warmers that allowed them to go down on one knee and shoot for hours without feeling the cold.

Soviet strategy was simple. Stalin planned to smash the Finns with gigantic sledgehammer blows. Masses of troops supported by armor and aircraft would be hurled at the outnumbered Finns. They'd smash their defenses, take their cities, and dictate peace terms in Helsinki, the Finnish capital. It wasn't a matter of military genius or luck, just brute force applied without mercy.

Thursday, November 30, 1939. Dawn. The Finns knew they were at war when sirens wailed in Helsinki. As people ran to shelters, scores of two-engined Ilyushin bombers soared overhead. Banking, the doors in their bellies opened and they began their bomb runs. Clusters of fire bombs and high explosives whistled as they sped earthward. The air became filled with the sound of explosions and collapsing buildings. Above the din came the clang of fire engines racing to their destinations. Everywhere there were burning buildings, the odor of burnt flesh, and the cries of the injured. Two hundred civilians died, but it would have been worse had the Red flyers been more experienced.

Meanwhile, on the Mannerheim Line, troops saw rockets arch into the leaden sky and, reaching altitude, open like giant green blossoms of light. Suddenly hundreds of Soviet cannon opened fire. Moments later the troops heard a high-pitched SCREECH. Incoming shells!

All hell broke loose. Some shells, bursting above the tree-tops, sprayed red-hot shrapnel. Other shells hit the ground, sending domes of earth and rock leaping skyward. Snow-laden trees shook and fell, creating miniature blizzards. Sometimes, when a shell landed fifty yards away, a soldier felt the suction of the explosion pulling the boots off his feet; if lucky, that was all it pulled off. The unlucky had arms, legs, and heads torn off. Yet there was no panic; even the badly wounded gritted their teeth and dragged themselves off to a dressing station or waited patiently for the medics.

The bombardment continued for a half hour along the entire Mannerheim Line when it suddenly stopped. Another flare arched skyward and burst green. The Soviet infantry were coming.

The Finns were amazed at what they saw. Soviet tanks clattered across the frozen ground, followed by infantry shouting their war cry. *"Urra! Urra!"* Hurrah! Hurrah! The soldiers had never seen such a show of military might, not even in parades. A youngster shook his head and blurted out: "So many Russians—where will we bury them all?" His wisecrack spread from squad to squad, company to company, until it became the unofficial motto of the Finnish army. The hated Red Army became known as the "moving zoo."

But where was the Finnish Army? The Soviets seemed to be marching into a deserted world. Not a Finn was to be seen anywhere. Each Finn wore white from his head to his boots and lay under a white sheet, invisible in the snow, waiting. White-clad machine-gunners crouched in trenches or amid snow drifts, waiting.

On November 30 and in the weeks that followed, the Reds learned that the enemy was no pushover. The Finns, said an officer, weren't men but demons, maniacs, who feared nothing. When they did show themselves, they "fought like dead men"—soldiers who already considered themselves dead and wanted to take some of the invaders with them.

Since there were so few antitank guns, the Finns had to find other ways of dealing with the steel monsters. They invented the "Molotov cocktail," named after Soviet foreign minister Vyacheslav Molotov, one of Stalin's chief henchmen. The "drink" was a mixture of kerosene, tar, and gasoline in a whiskey bottle with a gasoline-soaked rag wrapped around its neck.

Using the Molotov cocktail involved a grim struggle of man against tank, flesh against steel. As a tank lurched onward, a white-clad man lit the gasoline-soaked rag and leaped from cover. Dodging bullets, he threw the bomb at the tank's air intakes or open hatches. The bomb burst, squirting liquid fire into every corner of the tank. Its crew, their hair and clothes burning, leaped out, only to be shot by Finnish riflemen. The Finns also cut holes in the ice of frozen lakes and planted floating mines, which bobbed against the new ice that formed. The pressure of a tank passing overhead exploded the mine, sending tank and crew to a watery grave.

The Red infantry discovered that the Finns were masters at setting booby traps. A line of troops might walk along a trail, not noticing a thin wire tangled among some twigs. BANG! Bloody pieces of two or three men splattered against a tree trunk. Men vanished in an orange flash when opening a barn door, walking onto a bridge, or kicking a dead cow. A soldier lost a leg when he stepped into manure. After two weeks in Karelia, the invaders were stalled in their tracks. Yet they were lucky, compared to their comrades in the north.

There were no trenches or barricades from Lake Ladoga to Petsamo on the Arctic Ocean. Although greatly outnumbered there, the Finns had the advantage in the endless forests and snow plains. Red columns twenty miles long crawled through this wilderness covering only two or three miles a day. Mountainous snowdrifts barred their way, causing long delays. Trucks skidded and men became exhausted trying to walk through the deep snow. There was no protection or scouting from above, since aircraft couldn't see under the forest canopy; patrols dared not leave the main trails for fear of *bielaja smjert*—white death.

Death was all around, ever-watchful and cunning. The long darkness of the winter nights and the wind in the trees masked incoming dangers. Sentries couldn't hear the swishing of skis, or see men in white gliding toward them with submachine guns slung across their backs. Small groups of Finns skied in among the enemy, shooting men and blowing up equipment. By the time the Red officers recovered from their surprise, the raiders had vanished into the gloom.

The forest never slept. Trees and boulders cast eerie shadows on the snow. Keen eyes, snipers' eyes, peered from the shadows. The slightest movement on the enemy side drew their attention—and a bullet. Finland's ace sniper was Simo Häyhä, a small, quiet man who'd won prizes for marksmanship before the war. Häyhä would slip out each day by himself to "hunt Russians." He killed over five hundred of them before being seriously wounded.

Hit-and-run tactics tore Soviet divisions into shreds, forcing them to withdraw for reorganization. Sometimes divisions like the 44th ventured too far into the forest and were cut off. They were wiped out by cold, hunger, and bullets. An eyewitness reported:

> The Russian debacle was ghastly. . . . For four miles the road and forest were strewn with the bodies of men and horses; with wrecked tanks, field kitchens, trucks,

gun-carriages, maps, books, and articles of clothing. The corpses were frozen as hard as petrified wood and the color of the skin was mahogany. Some of the bodies were piled on top of each other like a heap of rubbish, covered only by a merciful blanket of snow; others were sprawled against the trees in grotesque attitudes. All were frozen in the positions in which they died.

The Soviets fared as poorly in the air as on the ground. When the war began, Finland had 162 ancient planes to oppose an air fleet of 3,000 bombers and fighters. But what the Finns lacked in numbers, they made up for in skill and daring. Combat patrols with skull-and-crossbone markings on their wings would cruise high in the gray sky, looking for prey. Sooner or later they'd sight a formation of Soviet bombers flying from bases in Estonia. Sitting ducks.

The Finns dove, engines screaming, machine guns chattering. Whole squadrons fell over Finland, their courses marked only by the charred skeletons of planes and men. One pilot set a world's record for the most kills in the shortest time. On January 6, 1940, Lieutenant Sarvanto dove into a formation of seven bombers, downing six within four minutes; a comrade finished off the seventh. Altogether Finnish airmen destroyed between 850 and 1,000 Soviet planes in two months, losing 62 of their own aircraft.

Finland's resistance stirred the hearts of freedom-loving people everywhere. Although foreign governments remained neutral, their citizens helped privately. Americans collected money for Finnish women and children forced to flee to neighboring Sweden; the trains that brought them there were often machine-gunned by the Soviets. Europeans, especially Scandinavians, volunteered for military service. Over 8,000 Swedes skied across the border, joining hundreds of Norwegians and

Danes. Frenchmen, Englishmen, and Belgians took passage to Finland. Even Italians fought alongside the gallant Finns.

Stalin became furious as battle reports piled up on his desk. At dinner one night he insulted War Minister Voroshilov, blaming the disasters on him and his blundering generals. Voroshilov, who'd been at Stalin's side since the Revolution, lost his temper. Leaping up, he shouted into the dictator's face: "You have yourself to blame for all this! You're the one who had our best generals killed!" Then, to make his point, Voroshilov picked up a platter of meat and slammed it on the table. Amazingly, he survived to become president of the U.S.S.R.

Stalin decided to teach the Finns a lesson they'd always remember. After shooting several commanders for failing, he sent Marshal Timoshenko to the front. Timoshenko left nothing to chance. His army of 600,000 was reequipped with winter gear and automatic weapons. Masses of artillery were lined up wheel to wheel. Timoshenko meant to blow the Mannerheim Line sky-high.

The assault began on February 1, 1940, with air strikes larger than any seen during Hitler's blitzkrieg in Poland. Waves of bombers, ignoring frightful losses, pulverized Finnish supply lines. Below, artillery kept up a steady bombardment. In one day over 300,000 shells fell on the Mannerheim Line. After a week of this, green flares went up and the infantry stepped out. The Finns mowed them down like wheat before the scythe. But they were exhausted from lack of sleep and their ammunition was running out. There was nothing to do but ask Stalin for peace terms.

He wasn't generous. In order to save their country, the Finns had to give up the Karelian Isthmus, Petsamo, and more. When the people learned the price of peace, they flew the flags at half-mast in mourning. As the troops skied home from the front, many wept. They'd lost, although magnificently and with honor. Some 25,000 Finns had died, but they'd made the enemy pay an awful price. The Winter War cost the Soviets at least 250,000 killed, 2,300 tanks and armored cars destroyed, plus countless trucks, horses, munitions, and other equipment.

Saddest of all, perhaps, were the 30,000 Soviet prisoners of war. These men were terrified of being sent back, and with good reason. Stalin couldn't imagine that anyone who'd escaped his control for even a brief while—who'd learned what life was like outside Russia—would not turn traitor. Of course, he might be innocent, but Stalin, cautious man that he was, couldn't afford to take the chance. During the purge, Comintern agents and advisers who'd served in Spain were shot. As an added precaution, every Russian soldier captured during the First World War was sent to the *gulag*, since they might have been recruited to spy for Germany. Prisoners returning from the Winter War were the first to learn how Stalin treated his unsuccessful soldiers.

They were greeted with bands and handshakes at the border. During a victory parade in Leningrad they marched under banners with the slogan "The Fatherland Greets Its Heroes." They were marched through the city to railroad sidings, put on trains, and hauled away to slave labor camps. A man's war record meant nothing. Hero or coward, officer or private, all were equal in Stalin's eyes and shared the same fate.

While the Winter War raged, the "Phony War" was in full swing along the Western Front. You couldn't tell that Great Britain and France had been at war with Germany since the invasion of Poland. Both sides faced each other along the border from Belgium to Switzerland. Loudspeakers blared propaganda blaming the other side for the war. But no shots were fired.

Stalin was Hitler's faithful friend during the Phony War. Hitler's war machine needed more food and raw materials than Germany could supply on its own, especially after the British navy blockaded her ports. The U.S.S.R. sent vast amounts of valuable supplies to fill the gaps: 1.5 million tons of grain, 865,000 tons of oil, 101,000 tons of cotton, tens of thousands of tons of chromium, copper, and other minerals. To evade the blockade, the U.S.S.R. purchased raw materials in the Middle East and South America for shipment to Germany via the Mediterranean and Leningrad. Rubber was bought in Asia and sent to Germany by express trains over the Trans-Siberian Railway. In return the U.S.S.R. received aircraft engines, warship planes, and torpedoes.

Stalin aided Hitler's police and military in various ways. The NKVD handed over to the Gestapo eight hundred anti-Nazi Germans who'd fled to the U.S.S.R., including Communists. Nazi warships were allowed to take refuge and refuel in Soviet ports. Several times cruisers raiding Allied shipping ducked into Murmansk on the Arctic Ocean when British warships came too close. Stalin even allowed the Germans to build a naval base on Soviet soil. "Basis Nord," 35 miles northwest of Murmansk, was used for refitting German submarines and stockpiling supplies.

The Soviet government and Comintern did Hitler's dirty work wherever they could. They were most effective in France, which had a large Communist Party and important Communist-controlled labor unions. Acting on Moscow's orders, French Communists tried to stab their own country in the back. They denounced the government as "capitalist stooges," insisting that France's ally, Great Britain, wanted to "fight to the last Frenchman." Communists sabotaged defense factories and called strikes in key industries. Many of the leaflets handed out by Communists at factory gates had been printed in Germany and smuggled across the border.

The Phony War became a real war on April 9, 1940, when Hitler unleashed his blitzkrieg in the West. Armored spearheads, fueled in part with oil from Baku, drove deep into enemy territory. Paratroops dropped from the sky, firing bullets tipped with Soviet lead. The spring was mild, the sun shining brightly as Nazi troops decorated their helmets with wildflowers and sang cheerful songs. Victory was in the air; they could feel it, taste it. They took Denmark and Norway in a day. Holland was overrun in five days, Belgium in eighteen, Luxembourg in an hour. One proud capital after another echoed to their jackboots. And always there were the hoarse shouts of *"Sieg Heil! Sieg Heil!"* Hail Victory! Hail Victory!

France, which had halted the German advance in the First World War, collapsed in six weeks, thanks in part to the French Communist Party. As the invaders drove deeper into the country, strikes increased in the factories and on the railroads. French Communist Party chief Maurice Thorez broadcast from Moscow urging soldiers to desert. When the Germans marched into certain sections of Paris, they were greeted with red flags and cries of "Comrade!" The French Communist Party helped the Gestapo with lists of those who might resist the occupation.

Within weeks of the fall of France, Hitler began preparing for the invasion of Great Britain. Shipping was gathered in ports from Norway to Spain and troops drilled in landing exercises. The Luftwaffe, Germany's air force, started bombing British defenses to soften them up for the final blow. Each day for weeks on end, formations of Heinkel bombers and Messerschmitt fighters soared over the English Channel. They attacked not only air bases and arms factories, but civilians in their homes. The city of Coventry was nearly wiped off the map. London was "blitzed," struck by man-made lightning in the form of tons of high explosive and incendiary bombs. The planners of these raids were often helped by weather information supplied by the Soviets.

During 1940 and 1941, the British depended on the United States for much of their food and many of their weapons. President Franklin D. Roosevelt wanted to make his country the "arsenal of democracy." The British, he believed, were fighting America's battle. If they fell, democracy in Europe, possibly even the world, would be doomed. The only way to prevent this was to help the British defend themselves in every way possible. Thus, in March 1941, Congress passed the Lend-Lease Act allowing the president to lend, lease, sell, or give any war materials he saw fit to any government whose defense he thought vital to the security of the United States.

But Hitler's friend in Moscow had other ideas. Stalin ordered the Comintern and the American Communist Party to sabotage aid to Britain. Suddenly groups sprang up with names like Peace Mobilization Committee, Mothers' Day Peace Council, Peace Committee of the Medical Profession, and American Peace Mobilization. They were all Communist fronts. Front organizations in universities demonstrated against "British imperialism." During a 1940 "march on Washington," demonstrators chanted, "The Yanks are *not* coming" to help Europe as they'd done in the First World War.

Most dangerous of all, Communist-controlled unions struck in vital defense industries. Their leaders would take a genuine grievance such as poor wages or working conditions and use it to stir up trouble. Most strikers were patriotic Americans who didn't realize how they were being manipulated.

Yet the strikes were costly. A seventy-six-day strike in 1941 crippled the Allis-Chalmers plant in West Allis, Wisconsin, a major producer of equipment for building destroyers and submarines. California, which accounted for half of all U.S. aircraft production, was a prime target. The Vultee Aircraft plant at Downey and North American Aviation's plant at Inglewood were hit hard by strikes in 1941.

Despite strikes and demonstrations, American aid saved Britain during the critical years 1940–1941. In October 1940, Hitler cancelled the invasion, although air raids continued for months afterward. Now a new word was heard in the planning sections of the German High Command: Barbarossa. Barbarossa—"Redbeard"—was Hitler's code name for the attack on the U.S.S.R.

Stalin had been wrong about everything. Wrong about helping Hitler's rise to power. Wrong about the Finns being a pushover. Wrong about Germany and the Allies exhausting themselves in a long, costly war. Wrong about buying Hitler's friendship. And now the Soviet people would pay for his errors in blood.

THE GREAT PATRIOTIC WAR

HITLER, LIKE STALIN, BELIEVED THE ENDS JUSTIFIED THE MEANS. His diplomats might smile at the Soviet tyrant and sign treaties with him, but these were merely means to an end. And Hitler was perfectly clear about that end in *Mein Kampf*: "Nothing will ever prevent me from attacking Russia after I have achieved my aims in the West." He had to attack, because in his madness, he saw the U.S.S.R. as the home of "Jewish-Marxism," the greatest evil of all time.

This war would not be like the one in the West, where prisoners were spared—usually. The Nazi leader had a name for this type of war: *Vernichtungskampf*, a war of extermination. When the time came, most of the U.S.S.R.'s population would be killed and the survivors enslaved. "The [Russians] are to work for us," said Luftwaffe chief Hermann Goering, echoing his Fuehrer. "In so far as we don't need them, they may die."

Hitler had reason to be encouraged. The U.S.S.R. seemed a hollow shell, thanks to Stalin's destruction of a generation of military leaders. True, the Red Army outnumbered his own forces in most areas. It had nearly four million men in European Russia and another two million in Asia. Its tank force of 15,000, larger than all other nations' combined, was backed by 8,500–10,000 combat planes. But the Soviet's showing in the Winter War hardly inspired the Germans with fear. Those who'd studied that war laughed at the fumbling of Stalin's commanders.

The Fuehrer decided that eight weeks would be enough to

smash the Soviets. The end of the U.S.S.R. would allow him to send all his forces against Great Britain. And with Britain defeated . . . ? Why, he might go on to conquer the world.

The Nazi buildup continued throughout the spring of 1941. Each day tanks rolled eastward, until 3,400 were massed from the Baltic to the Black Sea, together with 7,200 pieces of artillery. These were supported by 600,000 motor vehicles of all types: trucks, motorcycles, armored cars, staff cars, communications vans, tankers, mobile machine shops. Some 3,000 planes waited at secret airfields under camouflage nets. Troops came on foot and in truck convoys. Civilians said they looked like jungle cats; in addition to a gray-green uniform, each soldier wore a camouflage cape with splashes of yellow, green, brown, and black. Of the 3.5 million men gathered for the assault, a million belonged to Hitler's Hungarian and Rumanian allies. Movements were made at night, as Hitler meant to catch the enemy by surprise.

Stalin shouldn't have been surprised. For months Soviet spies had reported the buildup and given the approximate date of the attack. German planes were spotted over Soviet territory, photographing airfields and other military installations. When one of these planes crash-landed, Stalin ordered it returned, together with the rolls of film found on board. At the last moment a German soldier named Albert Liskof deserted to the Soviets with news that the invasion would begin in four hours: 4:00 A.M., Sunday, June 22, 1941.

Stalin ignored all warnings; indeed, officers were shot for suggesting that an invasion was near, as if firing squads could change unpleasant facts. We cannot be certain why someone who distrusted his closest advisers should have trusted Hitler, who'd broken every one of his agreements. Perhaps he *needed* to believe the Fuehrer. Perhaps, realizing his errors, he became frightened and closed his mind to facts, hoping things would work out for the best. He knew his country was unprepared for a major war, a war which could bring the end of Communism. But whatever the reason, as the minutes of peace ticked away, the U.S.S.R.'s defenders slept in their barracks. They were rudely awakened.

Stalin awoke in his dacha outside Moscow to learn that Hitler's armies were blasting their way eastward. He had the bringer of the bad news shot immediately.

Rather than meet the crisis head-on, the Man of Steel panicked. During most of that morning he locked himself in his room, drinking glass after glass of vodka. He even refused to allow his troops to offer any resistance. When a field commander asked permission to return enemy fire, Marshal Timoshenko telephoned from Red Army headquarters: "I am informing you . . . that comrade Stalin has not authorized artillery fire against the Germans." The general, puzzled and angry, shouted, "How can that be! Our troops are being forced to retreat. Cities are burning and people are dying." Timoshenko replied firmly that he must not take defensive action.

Hitler began Barbarossa with air strikes deep inside Soviet territory. Nazi airmen visited every airfield within range of the front. They were amazed to find Soviet planes, hundreds of them, parked wingtip to wingtip in neat rows. Machine guns chattered, bombs whistled, leaving behind heaps of smoking, tangled wreckage. Planes not destroyed on the ground were easily shot down. A German veteran described the early air battles as "infanticide," the killing of infants, for the Red pilots hadn't improved much since the Winter War. The Germans boasted of having destroyed 1,200 planes in the first day's fighting, more than 6,000 by mid-July.

The Reds fared no better on the ground. Imagine a pair of ice tongs slicing through a block of butter to encircle a large chunk between their arms. Now imagine three sets of tongs with arms hundreds of miles long. Those were the Germans advancing in three main units, or army groups. Each army group's "arms" consisted of tanks and mobile artillery followed by troops moving under an umbrella of fighter planes. They thrust across the sunbaked plains, slicing through Soviet defenses and encircling vast numbers of enemy soldiers. Using these tactics, they captured 300,000 Red Army men at Minsk, plus 2,500 tanks and thousands of tons of supplies. And Minsk was just the beginning.

With the Red Army in retreat, the NKVD swung into action. Not that its troops went to the front. The NKVD, always at its best against the defenseless, had no intention of facing armed men who'd shoot back. As the Germans neared a city, the local NKVD paused only long enough to pile its loot into trucks, burn its files, and "clean out" the jails.

The clean-out began in the Baltic states. When Stalin took over these countries, he'd filled the jails with those who might be disloyal to their Red masters. The outbreak of war was their death sentence. To prevent their being freed by the Germans, prisoners were shot individually or machine-gunned in batches. To save time, NKVD guards threw hand grenades into crowded cells. In several places people were locked in their cells and the jails set on fire.

In the U.S.S.R. itself, the NKVD went on a murder spree. Gulag prisoners who couldn't be evacuated were simply killed. As the Germans neared the Olginskaya camp, for example, thousands of slave laborers were shot. One of the worst massacres took place in Lvov. It horrified even the Germans, able killers in their own right. When they arrived, the air was sour with the stench of rotting flesh and hummed with millions of flies. Lvov's three prisons were just slaughterhouses for human beings. Bodies were everywhere, shot, stabbed, torn to bits. Among them was the naked body of a girl, aged about eight, hanging by a towel from a ceiling lamp. The prisons' cellars were nauseating. "The cellars in question," said an official report, "had ceilings that were splashed with blood, and in [another room] the floor was covered with a layer of dried blood that was 20 centimeters [about 8 inches] deep. The bolshevik hangmen had literally waded in blood."

Stalin had reason to doubt the loyalty of his own people. The invasion was welcomed by those with grudges against either Stalin or Communism, or both. News of Red Army defeats raced through the gulag like wildfire. There millions of slaves were so miserable that they hoped for deliverance even at the point of Nazi bayonets. "They are coming!" prisoners whispered, knowing that to be overheard by a guard meant death. Still they whispered, and hoped, ignorant of the "deliverance" Hitler planned for them.

Elsewhere, the Germans were greeted warmly. Memories of the collectivization and famine of the 1930s were still raw wounds for millions of people. Now they had their chance to strike back at the tyrant in the Kremlin. In the Ukraine and White Russia, laughing villagers greeted German tank columns, offering bread, salt, and flowers, traditional gifts for honored guests. Cossacks fell on their knees before swastika flags, praying for a Nazi victory and for Stalin to go to hell.

Communism disappeared overnight in hundreds of villages. Communist Party officials and their families were thrown out of their homes and often beaten to death by vengeful peasants. Collective farms vanished as the peasants took back their land and farm animals.

People helped their German "liberators" in many ways. They gladly gave them food and, more importantly, information about Soviet positions and troop movements. Some villagers turned in downed Soviet airmen, gagged and tied. People even volunteered to fight alongside the Germans. At one time or another, nearly 400,000 Russians served in Hitler's armies, the first time large numbers of Russian citizens joined a foreign enemy. Some of the bravest fighters were the Cossacks, whose families followed close behind their units in wagons.

We can only guess how things would have gone had Hitler treated his new subjects humanely. Not thousands, but millions might have rallied to the Nazis and changed the course of history. But Hitler, too, was a slave—a slave to his own madness and hatred. He'd come to Russia not to liberate, but to exterminate and enslave. And that's exactly what he did.

People in the occupied areas soon realized that they'd exchanged one tyranny for another. Once the Germans were firmly in control, they showed their true colors. Everything of value was looted either for the soldiers' own use or to be sent home. Men and women were put to forced labor, repairing roads and bridges, digging antitank ditches. Others were deported to Germany as slave laborers, to die from beatings, overwork, and starvation. Any protest brought a bullet or a bayonet thrust.

The occupation was especially hard on the Jews. As in Poland earlier, Russia's Jews were singled out for "special treatment." It was always the same. When a town fell, the Jews were rounded up and killed. Entire communities, tens of thousands of men and women, young and old, disappeared without a trace.

One of the worst atrocities took place at Babi Yar, a ravine outside Kiev, the capital of the Ukraine. On September 28 and 29, 1941, 33,771 Jews were brought to Babi Yar by the SS, Hitler's special Security Service. A German described what happened:

> The people who got off the trucks, men, women and children of every age, had to undress on orders from an SS man who held a riding whip or dog whip in his

hand. They had to deposit their clothing, shoes, outer and underclothes separately, at certain places. . . . Without an outcry or weeping these people undressed, stood together in family groups, kissed and said goodbye to each other, and waited for the beckoning gesture of another SS man who stood at the pit and likewise held a whip in his hand.

During the quarter of an hour that I stood by the pit, I heard no laments or pleas for mercy. I observed a family of some eight persons. . . . An old woman with snow-white hair held a year-old baby in her arms and sang something to it and tickled it. The child crowed with pleasure. The couple looked on with tears in their eyes. The father held a boy of about ten by the hand and spoke comfortingly to him in a low voice. The boy was fighting back the tears. The father pointed his finger up at the sky, caressed his head, and seemed to be explaining something to him.

At this point the SS man at the pit called out something to his fellow. The other man divided off about twenty persons and instructed them to go behind the mound of earth. The family I have been speaking of was among them. . . .

The completely naked people walked down a flight of steps that had been cut into the earthen wall of the pit, stumbl[ing] over the heads of those who were already lying there. . . . They lay down in front of the dead and wounded; some stroked those who were still living and murmured what seemed to be words of comfort. Then I heard a series of shots.

Such crimes drove people into Stalin's arms. It had nothing to do with love of the tyrant or Communism. The issue was survival. Millions came to realize that, bad as it was, the Soviet government was their own. Life under it was dangerous and harsh, but at least they had a chance to live; German rule meant certain death. That realization made them listen when Stalin called for a "Scorched Earth" campaign early in July 1941.

Scorched Earth meant just that: deliberately burning the country. Everything that might be useful to the Germans must be taken away or destroyed. Villages were to be burnt to deny the enemy shelter from the rain and, later, from winter's cold. Wells were to be filled in, mines flooded, and railroad tracks torn up. Nothing must remain for the invaders.

It was as Stalin ordered. By late summer, the Germans found themselves advancing into a man-made desert. All around them the night sky was lit by burning wheat fields. In village after village they found only charred rubble. Except for those unable to travel and stray dogs, the villages were deserted. Everyone else had fled to Soviet-held territory or to the guerrilla bands in the forests. These bands, often organized and supplied by the Red Army, operated behind enemy lines. By day they hid from patrols and scout planes. At night they struck—hard.

Nothing German was safe from the guerrillas. Patrols were ambushed, trains derailed, and ammunition dumps dynamited. In this war the guerrillas could be as merciless as their enemy. They might poison the water supply of a German barracks and behead prisoners to strike terror into their comrades when they found them. Girls took German lovers, then put bombs under their beds. One night guerrillas derailed a hospital train and burned the wounded alive. Russian traitors and their families were destroyed like vermin.

Hitler declared the guerrillas "bandits" and ordered stern countermeasures. A hundred Russian civilians were to be executed for each German killed behind the lines. SS troopers carried out manhunts in which harmless civilians as well as guerrillas were slaughtered. Although most victims remain nameless, one is still honored today. Zoya Kosmodemyanskaya was a high school girl and member of the Communist Youth. One night her band cut German telegraph lines and set fire to an ammunition dump. Zoya was caught and executed. A photo of her hanging on the gallows gave people a focus for their anger and strengthened their determination to go on fighting.

The guerrilla war, which Hitler had provoked, backfired, handing him his first setback. Others soon followed.

Each of the army groups that invaded the U.S.S.R. had a special mission. Army Group North was to clear the Baltic states and encircle Leningrad, which was not to be captured but destroyed and its people massacred. Army Group South aimed at the Ukraine, the nation's breadbasket. Army Group Center, the largest and best equipped with tanks, was to take Moscow, the hub of the Soviet railroad network and a center of heavy industry. Moscow was the key to the war in 1941. Its loss would have split the U.S.S.R. in half, paralyzing Stalin's armies on the other two fronts.

The German plan worked magnificently, especially on the central front, where tank units took Smolensk and began rolling toward Moscow, 200 miles to the east. The troops were tired but cheerful, for, with Stalin's armies fleeing before them, victory was within reach. Then Hitler, the self-proclaimed "greatest military genius of all time," blundered.

In mid-July, he decided that Moscow could wait; it was his for the taking whenever he wished. Instead of giving the knockout blow, he sent most of Army Group Center's tanks to the northern and southern fronts. The drive on Moscow stalled, but Leningrad was cut off and most of the Ukraine fell. In three months he'd killed or captured 2.5 million Russian soldiers and destroyed all but 700 of their tanks. A happy Fuehrer announced over Radio Berlin that the Soviet enemy had been struck down and the army would return home after mopping-up operations. That's not what happened; for when he was ready to renew the drive on Moscow in September, things had changed.

Stalin was responsible for many of the changes. Once he got over his shock at the invasion, he took charge of the Stavka, or General Military Headquarters, the Red Army's high command. He was now supreme warlord as well as head of the Communist Party and the Soviet government. He took this job seriously. Unlike Hitler, who thought he knew everything and cursed his generals as "idiots" and "cowards," Stalin was willing to learn from others. He'd call a meeting to discuss battle reports, study maps, and hear recommendations. Stalin would ask a difficult question, then let his generals argue, sometimes using crude language, which he loved to hear. He'd sit there expressionless, puffing calmly on his pipe and absorbing every word. When he'd heard enough and weighed every argument, he decided. For better or worse, every important Soviet military decision of World War II was made by Joseph Stalin personally or with his knowledge and approval. In a real sense the war was his to win or to lose. Had he decided wrongly, he would have been blamed for the defeat. That the U.S.S.R. won was to his credit. But victory was purchased at a price that was unnecessarily high.

Stalin the warlord was utterly ruthless. Already feared, now his name was enough to make hardened combat officers shake in their shoes. Generals, their hair standing on end, stood at attention while speaking to him on the telephone. They knew that he'd break anyone who disappointed him. In the early days of the invasion, he had several generals shot and others sent to rot in the gulag.

Vanka—"Little Ivan"—the Russian common soldier, was

worse off under Stalin than under the tsars. Stalin saw Vanka, like the peasants and Five-Year Plan workers before him, not as a person, but as a cog in a machine. Whether he lived or died was no concern of Stalin's so long as he stopped the enemy and drove him back. He had none of the rights of soldiers in other armies; even the Japanese army, noted for its brutal discipline, was more humane. Vanka was the only soldier in modern times not to be given home leave. Medical attention was poor, and countless soldiers died of blood poisoning for want of antiseptics to clean simple wounds. Officers routinely cursed, kicked, and pistol-whipped him for the slightest infraction of the rules.

Vanka went into battle with guns at his front and back. Before him were the enemy's guns. Behind were the guns of SMERSH, special NKVD units assigned to all frontline areas. SMERSH, from *smert shpionam*, "death to spies," had two tasks: catching spies and policing Soviet forces. SMERSH watched everyone, from common soldiers to field marshals. Anyone who said the wrong thing, or might be *thinking* incorrectly, was arrested. SMERSH was also responsible for preventing retreats. When Stalin ordered troops to fight to the death, he meant just that. Fleeing troops were rounded up and put into punishment battalions to be used, and used up, as needed. During attacks, for example, these battalions were herded onto the battlefield and, with SMERSH machine-gunners crouching behind them, sent to draw enemy fire. Often they were marched into suspected minefields to clear the explosives with their lives. Stalin spoke the truth when he said, "In the Red Army it takes more courage to retreat than to advance."

It took even greater courage to surrender. Soviet prisoners of war were marked men the moment they gave up. The Germans treated captured horses better, since they needed horses and not "useless mouths" to feed. As a result, Russians were shot when captured or, worse, sent to prisoner-of-war cages, open fields circled with barbed wire and machine-gun towers. There, under the broiling sun, they died in droves. A Hungarian officer named Suylok recalled the horror of these cages:

> I woke up one morning and heard thousands of dogs howling in the distance. . . . I called my orderly and said: "Sandor, what is all this moaning and howling?" "Not far from here," he said, "there's a huge mass of Russian prisoners in the open air. There must be 80,000 of them. They're moaning because they are starving."
>
> I went to have a look. Behind wire there were tens of thousands of Russian prisoners. Many were on the point of expiring. Few could stand on their feet. Their faces were dried up and their eyes sunk deep in their sockets. Hundreds were dying every day, and those who had any strength left dumped them in a vast pit.

Of the 5.7 million Soviet prisoners of war, about 3.5 million, over fifty-seven percent, died in enemy captivity. No nation before or since has lost so many men after their surrender.

Stalin must share a good deal of the blame for this tragedy. During World War II, Soviet prisoners were the only ones abandoned by their government. This meant that no food, clothing, or medicine was sent to the prison camps from home. No provision was made for forwarding mail from loved ones. The International Red Cross was not asked to check on the welfare of captured Red Army men. They could have rotted for all Stalin cared.

Stalin, in fact, turned against them. As he had declared after the Winter War, there were no Soviet prisoners of war, only Soviet traitors. In September 1941, he made this official

*Red Army prisoners of war. These soldiers could
expect no help from their country, as Stalin
considered them all traitors.*

army policy, decreeing that soldiers were to kill themselves rather than be taken prisoner. Those who allowed themselves to be captured, or, being captured, escaped, would be branded traitors. And that brand could mark others. Their families could be deported to Siberia or, at the very least, have their rations cut. Ex-prisoners were arrested if they fell into Soviet hands. Two instances are known of Soviet planes bombing camps filled with Soviet captives. The bombers were followed by aircraft dropping leaflets reading: "So will it be with those who betray the cause of Lenin and Stalin."

Several weeks before the suicide order, a Soviet artillery lieutenant was captured. In going through his pockets, the Germans found that they had Yakov Djugashvili. Stalin and his elder son had never gotten along, and his capture didn't endear him to his father. Stalin was angry, not at the Germans, but at Yakov for allowing himself to be taken alive. He suspected that Yakov had "disgraced" himself on purpose in order to embarrass his father. When the Germans offered to exchange him for one of their generals, Stalin said he didn't exchange high-ranking officers for common soldiers. He let Yakov stay in a German prison camp until he was shot by the guards. Yakov's Jewish wife was imprisoned for two years on suspicion of having betrayed him to the Jew-killing Nazis.

Moscow, not his son's fate, filled Stalin's thoughts in the fall of 1941. By failing to capture Moscow when he could, Hitler gave Stalin an unexpected gift: time. Stalin used that time to turn the capital into a fortress. Its population was organized into labor battalions to dig trenches and set up barbed-wire entanglements. Antiaircraft batteries were set up in a wide belt around the city; other batteries protected Red Square and the Kremlin. Pillboxes and machine-gun nests were positioned to make the enemy fight for every foot of ground. NKVD engineers mined every important structure, since the capital was not immune from the Scorched Earth policy. If Moscow couldn't be held, Stalin would blow it up.

That proved unnecessary, because time began to work against the invaders. Resistance stiffened as Stalin threw hundreds of thousands of reservists, mostly untrained peasants, into the battle. These men, Germans wrote in letters home, fought like "devils." Men rushed tanks, sacrificing their lives to ram dynamite down the gun muzzle. The Molotov cocktail, used so effectively by the Finns, was adopted by the Russians with deadly effect. Pilots, their ammunition exhausted, deliberately rammed German planes or crashed into tanks.

The rains came in September, as they come to Russia every year. What had been a swift, easy advance became a slow, bloody test of willpower and stamina. Fields became lakes, unpaved roads swamps. Soldiers, soaked to the skin, stood waist deep in thick, sucking mud, trying to free trucks and field guns. A feeling of desperation began to grip the exhausted Germans. By October they were waking to find frost on the ground. Worse, there were occasional snow flurries. Snow! Winter was coming and they still wore summer uniforms.

The tide turned during two days in November. On November 17, a tank unit was attacked sixty miles from Moscow. It wasn't much of an attack, but it stunned the Germans. Thousands of horsemen charged out of a forest, shouting and waving swords. The Germans cut them down with machine guns and cannon without losing a man. When they examined the bodies, they found they weren't Europeans but Asiatics. Wiry little men with black hair and high cheekbones, they wore the insignia of the 44th Mongolian Cavalry Division. They were the vanguard of the army Stalin had ordered west from Siberia.

On November 19, winter arrived in its full fury. Winds roared out of the Arctic, dropping temperatures to − 50° Fahrenheit, while blizzards blanketed the land in white. The cold crippled Hitler's war machine. Tank engines froze and lubricating oil in weapons turned to black jelly. In order for planes to fly, their engines had to be run constantly, increasing breakdowns. If a soldier touched metal with an ungloved hand, then pulled it away, he left strips of his own flesh. Every day thousands came down with pneumonia, frostbite, and snow-blindness. The wounded, cemented to the ground by their frozen blood, fell asleep forever. Stalin, however, had learned something from the Finnish war; he made sure his troops had fur caps, quilted jackets, and felt boots.

Still the Germans clawed their way toward Moscow. Nearer and nearer they came. Sixty miles. Forty miles. Twenty miles. Stalin now made one of the most important decisions of the war. He realized that the people were looking to him for leadership. If he fled the capital, as so many others had already done, it would be a sure sign that the country was lost. But by staying, he would live up to his name, Man of Steel, showing the confidence that had failed him earlier. He stayed, and that news sent a thrill of hope through the U.S.S.R. "Stalin is in Moscow!" people told each other. "All is not lost! We can stop the Hitlerite beasts!" Stalin's example combined with winter and the arrival of the Siberians to halt the Germans. On December 7, after a German patrol saw the Kremlin's spires in the distance, they began their retreat.

At the same time, to the north, the Finns, out to avenge the Winter War, joined the Germans in the siege of Leningrad. Beginning on September 9, Leningrad was bombed from the air and shelled by the largest guns in Europe. Taking as their motto the World War I battlecry "They shall not pass," Leningrad's defenders, soldiers and civilians alike, resolved to fight to the death. Leningrad, like Moscow, was mined and would be blown up if the enemy broke through.

The siege resembled a scene from hell. Food supplies fell so low that hundreds of thousands died during the "Starvation Winter." Things became so bad that people thought themselves lucky to get a glob of boiled furniture glue or a piece of dog meat. Once again, people resorted to cannibalism. People, especially young children, whose flesh was valued for its taste and tenderness, were kidnapped and killed; there were places where one could buy patties made from their ground-up flesh. Not even the certainty of execution could prevent this grisly trade. "In the worst of the siege," a survivor recalled, "Leningrad was in the power of the cannibals. God alone knows what terrible scenes went on behind the walls of the apartments."

Although some food was trucked in over frozen Lake Ladoga, and a corridor was later cut through enemy lines, the siege continued for 900 days. When it ended, as many as 1.5 million Leningraders had died. They are buried in common graves in a vast cemetery outside the city, honored for their role during that terrible year of 1941.

That year, however, wasn't one only for fighting. Stalin, more firmly in control than ever, began to prepare for the life-and-death struggle that lay ahead. And the outcome of that struggle, called "The Great Patriotic War," would depend as much on what happened on the home front as on the battlefront.

Stalin's home-front effort blended propaganda and terror with hard work. In the early days of the war, he'd said "We shall never rouse the people to war with Marxism-Leninism alone." These ideas weren't emotional enough to fire up the masses. People needed to love their country passionately and to hate the enemy with blind fury. Thus for the first time since the Revolution Soviet propaganda praised the glories of "Mother Russia," who in the long run always defeated her enemies.

Posters, radio broadcasts, songs, and films urged the people to imitate the heroes of Russia's past, even though they'd served the tsars. *Alexander Nevsky*, one of the finest Russian movies ever made, was about the hero who defeated Germanic invaders in 1240. Another hero was Prince Mikhail Kutusov, leader of the Russian armies against the emperor Napoleon in 1812.

Hatred was easy to inspire, given German atrocities. The titles of two popular poems give an idea of this hatred: "Kill Him!" and "I Hate!" Novelist Ilya Ehrenburg, one of Stalin's favorite authors, called the Germans "gray-green slugs" and demanded "two eyes for an eye, a pool of blood for a drop of blood." The duty of every Russian was clear, Ehrenburg said: "Let us not speak. Let us not be indignant. Let us kill. . . . If you have killed one German, kill another. There is nothing jollier than German corpses."

Most of all, one had to be true to Stalin. Wartime propaganda showed him larger than life, a great, good, heroic leader who never made a mistake. Because of his genius, he was awarded—that is, he awarded himself—medals and military titles:

> Supreme Military Leader
> Marshal of the Soviet Union
> Hero of the Soviet Union
> Architect of Victory

Oil paintings show him scanning enemy positions with field glasses as admiring soldiers look on, although he never showed himself anywhere near the front.

Stalin, the atheist, also enlisted the Russian Orthodox Church in the war effort. Almost from the first day of the war, he made life easier for the church. It was like a miracle, as if the church had awakened from a twenty-four-year nightmare. Antireligious propaganda stopped completely; indeed, antireligious museums were closed, the League of the Militant Godless abolished, and its magazine, *The Atheist*, turned into a religious journal on Stalin's direct order. Persecution ended as priests were released from prison and parents were allowed to teach their children about God. Radio Moscow even began broadcasting a religious hour of sermons and music. The church, in gratitude, asked the faithful to give money to buy arms, care for the wounded, and help war widows and orphans. And, miracle of miracles, priests prayed for the health of Stalin, "our God-given leader."

But nothing changed in the gulag. It flourished as never before. As the war continued, the number of "crimes" punishable by slavery increased. "Defeatists"—anyone thinking out loud that the war was going badly—got ten years at hard labor, as did "rumor spreaders" and "radio criminals." Stalin had ordered all radios turned in to prevent people from hearing German propaganda; Soviet programs were broadcast over loudspeakers in factories and on street corners. It meant your life to disobey the radio law, as several learned when discovered with some old radio parts.

Entire nations were also uprooted at Stalin's command. These nations, though tiny, had their own languages and long, rich histories. The Volga Germans, descendants of Germans who'd settled in Russia in the eighteenth century, had a separate republic within the U.S.S.R. The Crimean Tartars, relatives of the Mongols, lived in the Crimea, a peninsula jutting into the Black Sea. The Chechins, Ingush, Balkars, and Karachai came from the Northern Caucasus. Suspecting they might become disloyal, Stalin had NKVD troops herd every one of them into freight cars. No fewer than one million people were thus swallowed by the gulag or exiled to Siberia and the far north.

Life for the ordinary worker, harsh in the best of times,

became harsher. Stalin used the fall and winter of 1941 to move factories far beyond the reach of German air power. During those critical months, 1,360 factories were dismantled and reassembled thousands of miles to the east, in the Urals and Siberia. One of the world's largest steel mills was dismantled, sent east in eight thousand boxcars, and put back into production within four months.

Workers and their families came along with their machines. When they arrived, they set up the machines in the open, and, while they worked, others built their factory around them, often during driving snowstorms. They got along as best they could, living in unheated shacks or holes in the ground roofed with tin.

Without protection from real unions, workers were at their bosses' mercy. For being a few minutes late, workers went to swift death in the gulag. Hundreds of young girls between the ages of eighteen and twenty drew six-to-eight-year prison terms. Country girls, they'd been drafted by the government to work in factories far from home. Unable to bear the hardships, or, learning that a parent was ill, some asked to return home for a few days. If permission was refused, and they took unexcused leave, they were arrested upon their return. Few saw their parents again.

Wartime hardships were not shared equally. As always, the privileged government and Communist Party officials lived better than the average Russian. They still shopped in special stores, wore fine clothes, and ate the best foods. While commonfolk got by with black bread and water, they still had plenty of wine, fresh fruit, and caviar. Some of the salmon they enjoyed was packed in Kolyma by slave girls dressed in flour sacks who worked fourteen hours a day gutting and packing the fish; the skin of their hands cracked and the salt seeped into the wounds.

Once industry was relocated, production soared. By 1942,

the U.S.S.R. was producing most of its own war supplies. Better yet, it produced masses of new weapons such as the T-34 tank, the best all-around tank to come out of World War II, and the Katyushka—"Little Kate"—a rocket launcher mounted on a truck.

Thousands of those trucks came from the capitalist democracies Stalin hated and had tried to help Hitler destroy. Now that Great Britain and, after Pearl Harbor (December 7, 1941), the United States were allied to the Soviets, they were generous in their aid. Ship convoys brought supplies to Murmansk on the Arctic Ocean and the White Sea port of Archangel. It was rough going for the merchant seamen, warriors without weapons. They were attacked constantly by enemy planes based in Norway. Bombs and bullets were bad enough, but the sea was deadliest. If not rescued immediately after falling into the icy water, a man became unconscious in a minute and died within five. Yet, because of them, the U.S.S.R. received seventeen million tons of supplies.* Those supplies would be needed in the battles that lay ahead.

Although Hitler had lost much equipment and 750,000 men killed and wounded in 1941, he was still determined to destroy "Jewish-Marxism." Once his forces dug into winter positions and cold-weather gear arrived, he began to repair the damage. Reserves were called up and rushed to the Eastern Front. War plants worked overtime to replace lost equipment. By spring 1942, teletypes in German headquarters in Russia began to tick out coded orders. Objective: Stalingrad.

Stalingrad was a symbol of the Soviet tyrant himself. During

* The Allies sent a total of 18,700 planes, 10,800 tanks, 9,600 cannon, and 427,284 trucks, in addition to locomotives, boxcars, machinery, and aviation fuel. Most of the trucks were driven to the U.S.S.R. by way of Iran.

the Civil War, as Tsaritsyn, Stalin had defended it against the Whites. Proud of his achievement, he'd renamed it "Stalin City" in tribute to himself. Modernized under the First Five-Year Plan, it became a model city of 500,000 whose factories made tractors for Soviet agriculture and tanks for the Red Army. But most of all, Stalingrad was on the west bank of the Volga, and that's what caught Hitler's eye.

His plan for 1942 depended on taking Stalingrad. Once the city fell, the attacking force would split in two. One part would sweep northward along the Volga, cutting off Moscow from the east. The other part would drive southward into the oil-rich Caucasus, bringing the Soviet war machine to a screeching halt for lack of fuel.

German tanks began to move on June 22, the first anniversary of Barbarossa. Their advance seemed like a repeat of the original invasion. For two months they slashed eastward, breaking through one defense line after another. By late August, they'd crossed the Don River, the last natural barrier before their objective. Stalingrad was shelled day and night. Bombers pounded it with high explosives, killing 40,000 people in a single raid. Hardly a building remained intact when the first tanks nosed their way into the ruined streets.

Stalin vowed to hold "his" city at any cost. Overall command of the Stalingrad front was given to Marshal Georgi K. Zhukov. A short, stocky man of forty-four, Zhukov had a bright smile and an explosive temper. A no-nonsense soldier, he'd organized Leningrad's defenses and planned the counterattacks around Moscow. He expected things to be done "right," that is, his way, and on time. Once, when a general said he couldn't move his troops on short notice, the smile faded from Zhukov's face. "Light dawns," he growled. "You better get your thinking cap on. If that division is not in position by 9:00 A.M. I'll have you shot." The troops were in position by 9:00 A.M.

Zhukov's plan for Stalingrad was simple. While his deputy, General Vasili I. Chuikov, pinned the Germans down in the city, he'd prepare a massive counteroffensive. His object was not merely to hold ground, but to destroy the attacking army completely.

Chuikov obeyed his orders to the letter. Throughout the summer and into the fall, he fought the Nazis amid the ruins of Stalingrad. Every street, every house, every room, attic, and cellar became a battlefield littered with dead men and discarded equipment. Typical of the Soviet effort was the defense of "Pavlov's House" in the center of the city. The house was held by twenty men led by Sergeant Yakov Pavlov. The Germans wanted that house—badly! For fifty days they blasted it and riddled it with machine-gun bullets. Pavlov held his house, piling up German corpses while a phonograph he'd found played the same record over and over again.

Zhukov, meantime, secretly gathered a million men to the north and south of the city. He, too, remembered anniversaries. On November 19, a year to the day after the 44th Mongolian Cavalry Division charged near Moscow, he struck. Now the Germans were on the receiving end of a blitzkrieg. Thousands of guns and Katyushka rockets began a bombardment that shook the ground for miles around. The bombardment slackened only as T-34 tanks lurched forward, followed by swarms of infantry.

The Germans were trapped and forced to spend the winter in the ruins of Stalingrad. As before, they had only summer uniforms, and the winter of 1942 was colder than usual. They froze, starved, and died painfully of infected wounds. When the end came on January 31, 1943, they'd suffered a stunning defeat. Lost were 61,000 vehicles, 8,000 guns, and 1,550 tanks. These could be replaced, but not the men to use them. Of the 280,000 soldiers trapped in Stalingrad, 91,000 surren-

Relocated far beyond the reach of the German advance, this factory in Siberia could produce a steady stream of bombs. Below, the once great city of Stalingrad, reduced to rubble by German shelling.

dered, among them one field marshal and twenty-four generals. For the next five months, they were marched to prison
camps in Siberia. Only 6,000 of these were to return home
after the war. The rest died, as Stalin's slaves had always died,
of beatings, overwork, disease, and starvation. The Soviet government has never released complete figures of its losses in
the Battle of Stalingrad, but they were certainly as large as the
enemy's.

A wise man would have learned the right lessons from Stalingrad. He would have decided that, since the Reds were stronger
than he'd expected, and getting stronger, he'd best retreat to
strong defensive positions and let them exhaust themselves in
costly attacks. That's what Hitler's generals advised, but Hitler
decided to gamble everything in another gigantic battle.

His objective was a salient, or bulge, in the Soviet line near
the city of Kursk. The Kursk salient, 70 miles long and 110
miles deep, was both a danger and a temptation. It was risky,
lying as it did at the hinge of Army Group Center and Army
Group South. Whenever the Reds wished, they could break
the hinge and strike at either group's flank, its long, exposed
side. But Hitler couldn't pass it up, for by attacking it from
the north and south, he might trap vast numbers of enemy
troops in a "pocket." He believed that such a victory would
undermine the Soviet will to fight and prove to the world that
Germany was still all-powerful.

On April 15, 1943, the Fuehrer gave the order to prepare
Operation Citadel, the Kursk offensive. Some of his best divisions were to assemble on either side of the salient. New
types of tanks were to be rushed to the area and kept under
cover until the day of battle. Surprise would be total—or so
Hitler thought. Stalin knew better.

Within a week, Moscow received a signal from "Lucy" in
Lucerne, Switzerland. "Lucy" was the code name of Rudolf

Roessler, a Soviet agent with friends in the German high command. To this day his friends' identities remain a mystery. But they must have hated Hitler and been eager to destroy him. Throughout the war, they passed top-secret information to Lucy, which Lucy broadcast to Moscow. Lucy's information was so valuable that his messages were always handed to Stalin personally.

Lucy's greatest service was the tip-off about Kursk. From April onward, his reports covered everything a war leader needed to know about the enemy. Lucy named the German commanders and their units; in time, Hitler would commit 570,000 men to Citadel. Lucy told about the Nazis' 3,000 tanks and assault guns, heavy cannon mounted on tank chassis. He carefully described the Tigers and Panthers, Hitler's newest tanks. The Tiger outweighed anything in the Soviet arsenal (56 versus 52 tons), had thicker armor, and carried a long-range gun. The Panther was Hitler's answer to the T-34, faster, heavier (49 versus 32 tons), and with a larger gun. There was also the Ferdinand, a dinosaur among fighting vehicles. This "tank destroyer" weighed 72 tons and mounted a gun with a 21-foot barrel. Hitler expected his hundred Ferdinands to roll over anything in their path.

Stalin had to decide how to use Lucy's information. He could attack, throwing the Germans off balance and forcing them to cancel Citadel. That would buy more time for a bigger Soviet buildup and an attack later in the year. Or he could let the Germans attack, weaken themselves, and then counterattack. This was the riskier course, for it meant that the Red Army, which had never won a summer campaign, would let the enemy strike first. But it was also the most rewarding course. If successful, it would tear the heart out of the German army. Stalin decided to wait for the German attack. To make sure things went well, he sent Georgi Zhukov to Kursk.

Zhukov secretly prepared a warm reception for the Germans. By the time his buildup was completed, the Kursk salient was defended by 977,000 troops, 3,300 tanks, and 20,000 guns, twice the enemy's firepower. Zhukov's combat engineers prepared six defense lines, one behind the other. The key to the defenses was the *Pakfronts* designed to deal with enemy tanks. Each Pakfront had up to ten antitank guns commanded by one officer, who'd fire them all at a single tank; they couldn't miss. The Pakfronts themselves were protected by infantry in trenches and machine-gunners with orders to shoot only at enemy foot soldiers. And, for good measure, minefields were planted in front of their positions. Kursk was a death trap waiting to snap shut.

The Battle of Kursk began on July 5, 1943. As a dawn haze burned off, Soviet lookouts saw the enemy massed to the north and south of the salient. There, amid tall grass and cornfields flecked with poppies, stood the flower of the German army. They were arranged in wedge-shaped formations, the better to drive themselves into the Soviet defenses. Each wedge was tipped with Tiger tanks. Behind them were Panthers and older, but still deadly, Mark IVs. The infantry came behind the armor in personnel carriers and on foot.

The Russians met them with a thunderous blast of fire. Thousands of cannon and Katyushkas spoke at once. The firing was so heavy that you couldn't hear a single gun, but only a continuous roar and crash. It was hard work and the artillerymen, stripped to the waist, became black as dust and smoke particles stuck to their sweaty skin.

The bombardment's effect was terrifying. Shells plowed the earth around the German tanks. Tank crews, hearing light shells bounce off harmlessly, gulped hard, thankful for good German steel. Others died as heavy shells split open their tanks like tin cans. Everywhere exploding shells set the grass and cornfields ablaze. Shrapnel filled the air with whining death.

As the German formations approached the Pakfronts, mines began to take their toll. Tanks, their treads blown away, stopped, becoming easy targets for the Red artillerymen. Their companions kept moving, only to be blasted by concentrated antitank gunfire. Red machine-gunners and riflemen mowed down exposed infantrymen in windrows. Wounded were everywhere, screaming, bleeding, dying amid noise and flame. The German veterans had never seen such mayhem. "Our medical staff were unable to cope with all the wounded," a corporal wrote home. "One medical orderly told me that the dressing station was like a slaughterhouse to look at."

Ninety Ferdinands went into action in the southern sector. Although they did well at first, they never really had a chance. Soviet troops were amazed as big shells bounced harmlessly off their armor and they rolled over exploding mines as if they were firecrackers. Their problems began only when they overran trenches. The Soviet troops didn't run away, but stayed behind until the Ferdinands passed. Then they clambered aboard from behind and poked the nozzles of flamethrowers into the ventilators. A squirt of liquid fire and the Ferdinand was finished, its crew burnt to cinders.

When the fighting ended at sundown, the Germans had little to show for their efforts. They'd punched a few miles into both sides of the salient and overrun some trenches, but at a tremendous cost in life and materiel. Reports noted 586 tanks crippled or destroyed in one day. Nor did things improve in the days that followed, when 433, 520, and 304 tanks were lost. Supplies, too, were running short. Guerrillas operating behind the lines played the devil with truck convoys and railroads. A German soldier wrote his wife: "With us trains move for one day and three days have to be spent repairing the tracks since the partisans blow everything up. The night before last they arranged a collision between an express train and a leave train. . . . That's the way we live in Russia."

Stalin followed every detail of the battle. By 1943, he'd given up any kind of a personal or family life. Running a huge country and a war at the same time took every ounce of his energy. When his daughter, Svetlana, asked permission to get married, he only snapped, "To hell with you, do what you like," and returned to his work. He never met her husband.

The climax at Kursk came on the southern front. On July 12, Soviet general Pavel A. Rotmistrov, commander of the Fifth Guards Tank Army, was at his headquarters at Prokhorovka overlooking a narrow road nestled between a small river and a steep railway embankment. Rotmistrov had planned to use his entire force of 850 tanks to strike the Germans at the other end of the road, which was invisible from his headquarters. At his signal, tankers started their engines and moved out at top speed. Moments later, 700 German tanks and self-propelled guns appeared. Unknown to each other, both sides had secretly launched all-out attacks at the same time and along the same road. And now 1,550 vehicles were racing toward each other for the greatest armored clash in history.

Ordinarily, the Tigers would have blasted the T-34s to junk with their long-range guns. Unfortunately for them, that strength was also a weakness. The Tiger was superior to the T-34 only when its gun could be aimed at a distant target. At close quarters, however, the T-34's smaller weapon was just as effective.

The Russians took full advantage of the Tiger's weakness. Engines roaring, they charged, eager to close with the enemy as quickly as possible; one German remembered T-34s "streaming like rats all over the battlefield." Amid heat and dust, steel monsters lurched and bounced, firing as targets came into view. The place became littered with blazing, broken tanks.

Often, when a tank was hit, its ammunition and fuel exploded, blowing off its turret and hurling it dozens of yards away.

The Russians fought with reckless courage. When Captain P. A. Skripkin's tank was set afire, his crew dragged him from the doomed vehicle. They were taking cover in a shell hole when a Tiger started to bear down on them. Without a word, Skripkin's driver ran back to the blazing tank, restarted the engine, and turned to meet the enemy. Thirty-two tons of steel and flame slammed into the Tiger, destroying both in a terrific explosion.

The battle was no less ferocious in the air. Both sides had sent up fleets of fighters to help their tanks. But since clouds of dust and smoke boiled up from the ground, making it impossible to tell friend from foe, the airmen went at each other in fierce dogfights. White parachutes blossomed against the sky. Planes trailing banners of fire streaked earthward, crashing amid the tanks.

When night came, there was no doubt about the victory. The Germans had lost half their force, while Rotmistrov still had at least 500 tanks in fighting condition. Hitler canceled Citadel the next day. The Americans and British had landed in Sicily on July 10—just before Citadel's final battle—and might soon invade Italy. The Fuehrer had to transfer large forces from the Eastern Front to the Mediterranean, to protect Italy.

The Battle of Kursk was a German disaster. Their losses were put at 70,000 men killed, plus 2,900 tanks, 1,049 guns, 1,392 planes, and over 5,000 motor vehicles; Soviet losses have never been revealed.

Kursk reversed the pattern of the war on the Eastern Front. Until Kursk, the Germans attacked and the Russians defended; it was Hitler who decided where to strike and when. Kursk ended the era of the German blitzkrieg. From then on, the Russians attacked and the Germans defended.

When the Germans retreated from Kursk, the Russians counterattacked along the entire Eastern Front. Their advance really was like a steamroller, slow, deliberate, irresistible, crushing everything in its path. Slowly but surely, they began to drive the enemy from Soviet soil. By the beginning of November 1943 the Red Army was back in Kharkov, the industrial capital of the Ukraine; Smolensk and Kiev were liberated after savage street fighting.

A self-assured Stalin arrived in Teheran, Iran, later that month for a conference of the "Big Three": himself, American president Franklin D. Roosevelt, and British prime minister Winston Churchill. During the discussions, Stalin promised an offensive in support of Operation Overlord, the Allied plan to invade France from across the English Channel and liberate Western Europe. Not that he was eager for Overlord to succeed too well. He had other plans for Western Europe, plans that had nothing to do with supporting democracy. Stalin hoped to succeed where Lenin had failed. The defeat of Nazi Germany was only his excuse for taking over Western Europe. Already Russians were being trained to govern the occupied countries. One man, for example, became an expert on Brussels, Belgium, another on the Berlin area, and so on. Once the Red Army set foot in the West, he meant to keep it there permanently.

Overlord began on "D-Day," June 6, 1944. The Americans and British landed on the French coast in Normandy and began a buildup of men and materiel for the drive inland. Meanwhile, as he'd promised at Teheran, Stalin launched a massive summer offensive across Eastern Europe. Rumania and Hungary were knocked out of the war; Finland made peace on Soviet terms.

The "Big Three," Winston Churchill, Franklin
D. Roosevelt, and Joseph Stalin, meet at Yalta
to plan Allied strategy as the war draws to a
close.

Stalin's legions swept across Poland and, by the end of July, were just across the Vistula River from Warsaw. The year before, the Jews of the Warsaw ghetto had risen against the Germans. Their revolt was crushed and the survivors sent to the gas chambers at Auschwitz. Now the Russians called for another revolt to help the Poles drive out the enemy. "Poles," said Radio Moscow, "the time for freedom approaches! Poles take to arms! There is not a second to lose! . . . People of Warsaw to arms! Throw out the German invader and take your freedom!"

On August 1, the people of Warsaw revolted. But the help they'd expected never came. While SS men shot the wounded in hospitals and made children march as shields in front of their tanks, the Red Army didn't budge. It sat across the Vistula, hearing the guns but doing nothing. The official explanation was that the army was low on supplies and had to be refitted. The truth, however, was not so simple. Stalin saw Warsaw as a chance to finish what he'd begun at Katyn. He knew that Polish patriots hated Communism and would never accept Soviet rule. They'd have to be killed, and who better for the job than the Nazis? Stalin's call for the Warsaw uprising was an invitation to suicide. After two months of fighting against hopeless odds, Polish resistance collapsed. Patriots were slaughtered by the thousands and Warsaw was almost completely destroyed. Then, and only then, did he send the Red Army across the Vistula.

Hitler's empire was crushed between the Soviet hammer and the Allied anvil. Wherever the Fuehrer turned, he saw enemies closing in. After D-Day, the Americans and British moved faster than Stalin expected, thus keeping the Red Army out of Western Europe. Next to the defeat of Germany, this was the Allies' greatest achievement of World War II, for it saved European democracy. On August 25, 1944, Paris was liberated. By March 1945, armored spearheads had crossed the Rhine River at Remagen and were plunging into the heart of Germany. Russian forces entered Germany from the east and headed for Berlin.

Every day German soldiers surrendered in droves to the Americans and British. But in the east they preferred to fight to the death. They had reason to fear capture by the Russians. Whether the Red Army "liberated" friends or foes, the result was always the same: a reign of terror.

Stalin's daughter tells us that he encouraged this terrorism and that it gave him pleasure. He wanted his soldiers to be hated so they couldn't become friendly with the local people and be "corrupted" by them. By "corrupted" he meant learning that others, even the hated Germans, were better off than they. When the Red Army broke into eastern Germany, troops were amazed to see peasants who had brick houses with running water and carpets. Their farm buildings were better than the Russian's own homes. Now terrorism would destroy a world that, after five years of war, still had a higher standard of living than the U.S.S.R. in peacetime.

Once inside Germany, generals allowed their men to run wild. Towns were looted and burned. Soldiers, for whom a wristwatch represented wealth and power, wore stolen watches in rows on both arms. There were also atrocities against the innocent as terrible as any committed by Hitler's soldiers. German women were raped wholesale. German children were shot for target practice or tossed live into burning buildings. A doctor saw where

> . . . a whole column of refugees had been rolled over
> by Russian tanks; not only the wagons and teams, but
> also a goodly number of civilians, mostly women and
> children, had been squashed flat by the tanks. . . . On

the edge of a street an old woman sat hunched up, killed by a bullet in the back of the neck. Not far away lay a baby of only a few months, killed by a shot at close range through the forehead . . . a number of men, with no other marks of fatal wounds, had been killed by blows with shovels and gun butts; their faces were completely smashed. At least one man was nailed to a barn door.

Surely their only crimes were being German and being in the wrong place at the wrong time.

The Red Army attacked Berlin during the last week of April 1945. On April 30, with rescue impossible and fighting raging only blocks from his headquarters, Adolf Hitler committed suicide. Berlin surrendered two days later and World War II ended in Europe.

Victory was celebrated with a huge parade in Red Square. Stalin stood atop Lenin's tomb to review the troops as an air armada droned overhead. His picture hung everywhere and loudspeakers blared his praises. Then, as a final tribute, Red Army men flung down hundreds of enemy battle flags at the foot of Lenin's tomb. Stalin smiled.

He had reason to smile. The Western Allies had fought well against Hitler's war machine, though it was pretty rough going in their Mediterranean and Western European campaigns. But they'd been fighting *less than half* of the German army. The rest was tied down in Russia. Stalin knew that the war couldn't have been won without Soviet help, and now he meant to enjoy the fruits of victory.

His people had paid a high price for that victory. Scholars estimate that fifty-five million people died in World War II. Of these, over twenty million, or thirty-eight percent, were Soviet citizens. By comparison, the United States lost 295,000 men, or seventy-two times less than the U.S.S.R. In addition, 1,700 Soviet towns and cities, 70,000 villages, and 32,000 factories and workshops were completely destroyed. No nation had ever taken such losses in war.

Yet the man in the Kremlin didn't consider this price too high. For the U.S.S.R. emerged from World War II as the greatest power on earth, second only to the United States. And therein lay the seeds of future conflicts.

INTO THE
SHADOWS

EARLY IN MAY 1945, TWO SIGNIFICANT, BUT SEEMINGLY CON-
tradictory events occurred. On May 9 the official announcement came over Radio Moscow that the war in Europe was
over. The news was expected, but when it came it triggered
an outburst of joy unknown in the Soviet capital. For the first
time since Stalin came to power, people gathered for a mass
demonstration that had not been staged by the government.
But instead of marching to the Kremlin, Muscovites by the
thousands poured into the square in front of the United States
Embassy. People cheered the Stars and Stripes and, whenever
an American appeared, lifted him and passed him, laughingly,
gently, over their heads. In their own way, ordinary people
were showing their appreciation of American generosity during
the war.

At about the same time, NKVD chief Beria's aide, Victor
Abakumov, spoke at a meeting of SMERSH officers. There
was nothing cheerful about his address. He spoke not of gratitude, but of hatred. "The British and Americans," he said,
". . . dream of lasting peace and building a democratic world
for all men. . . . All their slobber plays right into our hands,
and we shall thank them for this, in the next world, with coals
of fire. We shall drive them into such dead ends as they've
never dreamed of. We shall disrupt them and corrupt them
from within. The whole 'free western' world will burst apart
like a squashed toad. This won't happen tomorrow. To achieve
it will require great efforts on our part, great sacrifices. . . .
Our aim justifies all this. Our aim is a grand one, the destruc-

210

tion of the old, vile world." This was not just the raving of a lunatic. Abakumov spoke for Beria, and, as the SMERSH officers knew, Beria was merely Stalin's echo.

The Russian people were sick of war. After their struggle with Hitler, they wanted only to mourn their dead and rebuild their lives. They hoped that the industries created during the war would be turned to peaceful uses. They looked forward, not to the return of lines outside shops, but to enough food and clothing at fair prices. They wanted housing, education, and medical attention. They wanted to live in peace.

Stalin, however, had other priorities. The world may have changed since June 1941, but his ideas and desires remained the same. He was still a Communist, still a believer in world revolution. Most of all, he still believed in the mission of the U.S.S.R. to lead that revolution, conquering the world for Communism. Only now Stalin was an old man, with a weary body, tired eyes, and tobacco-stained teeth. Powerful as he was, even he couldn't live forever. But before he slipped into the shadows, he was determined to see a Communist world.

In the quiet of his Kremlin office, beneath the portrait of Karl Marx, Stalin planned for the future. He planned carefully, his orderly mind taking each step in logical sequence. First, there must be no more shows of appreciation for the capitalist democracies; the people must be made to hate everything foreign. Second, he must repair the war's damage and expand heavy industry. Third, he must create a series of "satellites" in Eastern and Central Europe to serve as a barrier against the democracies and as a launching pad for the final battle. "We shall recover in fifteen or twenty years," he'd say privately, "and then we'll have another go at it." Make no mistake about it: when all was ready, Stalin intended to launch World War III.

Stalin began by sealing off the U.S.S.R. as it had never

been sealed off before. His purpose was to cut off contact with foreigners, keeping his people ignorant of the world outside. Thus, without information, or with only the facts he wanted them to know, people would have only his version of the "truth." It was a well-thought-out program and, to a greater or lesser extent, operates in the U.S.S.R. down to the present day.

A key element in the program involved isolating foreigners living in the U.S.S.R. Isolation took various forms. Both the American and British embassies, whose windows overlooked the Kremlin, were relocated. Foreign diplomats, who in most countries may travel freely, could travel only among a few Soviet cities, and then only with official permission. Foreign journalists had to submit every article to censorship before it could be sent out of the country. The Decree on Revealing State Secrets made it a crime for Soviet citizens to tell foreigners about epidemics, reveal the type of goods produced in workshops, and mention airports and transport routes. Indeed, having anything to do with foreigners was "collaboration with the international bourgeoisie." A Russian could be, and often was, jailed for giving directions to an American on the street.

Stalin set out to erase every trace of foreign influence from people's minds. Rules against importing foreign publications were strengthened and more powerful equipment used to jam foreign radio broadcasts. The Russian language itself was purged of foreign words. Drugstores no longer sold "English salts" to treat stomachaches but "bitter salts." Bakeries changed "French bread" into "city bread."

Still the tyrant wasn't satisfied. In 1947, marriages between Soviet citizens and foreigners were forbidden by law with severe penalties. Hundreds of marriages, even ones made before the law went into effect, were tragically broken. A typical case involved a Russian woman who'd married an American doctor in Germany at the end of the war. After a few years in the United States, she decided to visit her aging parents. Surely, she thought, there was no harm in *that*. But no sooner did she arrive than she disappeared. After many appeals, her husband received permission to come to the U.S.S.R. to look for her. Arriving in Leningrad in 1951, he was arrested and sentenced to twenty-five years as a spy. He vanished into the gulag and was never heard from again.

In the meantime, Stalin ordered a propaganda campaign against the Western democracies as poisonous as anything during his alliance with Hitler. The democracies were condemned as "filthy imperialists" bent on enslaving humanity. They were ruled by "warmongers," arms manufacturers who wanted war to increase profits. Only the dear "Socialist Motherland," the U.S.S.R., wanted peace. Its every action, said Radio Moscow, was aimed at preserving world peace. When it built up its armed forces or stirred up revolution in other countries, it was always for the sake of "peaceful internationalism." When it overthrew neighboring governments, it did so for the sake of "progressive humanity."

Propaganda against the United States was loudest, for it was willing to use its wealth and power to oppose Soviet expansionism. Stalin had broken his promises about restoring democracy in Eastern Europe and, President Harry S Truman felt, had to be stopped to safeguard the West from totalitarianism. As a result, Stalin used every means to stir up hatred against the United States. Films, plays, songs, poems, and children's books portrayed the United States as a nation of cutthroats. Cartoons and posters depicted Uncle Sam as a hooknosed brute with claws reaching out to grasp the world. "Wall Street," site of the New York Stock Exchange, was the center of world capitalism and thus a synonym for evil.

Every day, before starting work, factory workers had to attend

An anti-United States poster from 1948. A
Soviet soldier warns Uncle Sam, portrayed as a
warmonger, not to start trouble. At the time,
Stalin himself was preparing for another war.

the *Pyatiminutki*, the "five minutes," a mini-lesson in hatred. Propagandists explained that the United States never acted for moral reasons, but only out of self-interest. Lend-Lease, for example, was only a businessman's way of profiting from the war. The United States, *Pravda* noted in hundreds of articles, was a land of unemployment where workers' lives meant less than scrap metal, which could be salvaged and used again. *Pravda*, of course, never mentioned the gulag's millions of "fully employed" slaves; or Soviet factories, with their NKVD offices; or Soviet labor unions, which served the government. Race prejudice was another propaganda theme. Blacks in the United States were shown as victims of segregation and bigotry, forced to live in poverty. That charge was true enough, although it ignored the growing civil rights movement. Soviet anti-Semitism and the deportation of entire nationalities were also conveniently ignored.

Stalin's propaganda showed Russia as superior to all other nations. Russians, it was said, had invented everything of value in the modern world, although foreigners took the credit for themselves. A few of the "Russian" inventions were: the steam engine, penicillin, radio and telegraph, the airplane, helicopter, and lighter-than-air balloon, the submarine, electric light bulb, and internal combustion engine. The Soviets still claim responsibility for many Western inventions. In 1987 they even took credit for the invention of baseball!

Not everyone, however, took the propaganda seriously. Some joked about the superiority of Soviet watches: "Soviet watches are the fastest in the world." "Russia," it was said, "is the elephant's natural habitat." The hundreds of agents employed in buying, copying, and stealing any useful Western scientific development also knew the foolishness of Russian claims. But wise people kept their jokes to a whisper, for being overheard could mean your life.

Meanwhile, Russia's own scientists learned the penalties for not believing as Stalin believed. In the mid-1940s, he began a witch-hunt to cleanse Soviet science of Western influence. Western science, he declared, was not science at all, but "bourgeois lying." Hundreds of historians, economists, philosophers, chemists, and language specialists lost their jobs for teaching "un-Marxist" theories.

Stalin even abolished one science entirely in the U.S.S.R.: genetics, the study of heredity. To Stalin this science was Western nonsense. He preferred the theories of a Soviet quack named Trofim D. Lysenko, who believed in the inheritance of acquired characteristics. He claimed, for example, that one could breed short-tailed rats by cutting off their tails for several generations. Stalin even believed Lysenko when he said that wheat could be changed into rye, pine trees into fir trees, simply by changing their growing conditions. As a result, Stalin halted all scientific work in genetics. Geneticists lost their jobs, some were jailed, and a few killed.

They were but a tiny fraction of those ruined in the crusade against Western influence. On Stalin's orders, new offenses were added to the Soviet Criminal Code, such as "Praise of American Technology," "Praise of American Democracy," and "Toadyism Toward the West." These offenses, silly as they may seem, were no laughing matter. Conviction meant up to fifteen years at hard labor.

The gulag flourished as it swallowed swarms of fresh victims. Nearly all these victims, estimated at 2,272,000 men, women, and children, were Soviet citizens handed over against their will by the Americans and British. These unfortunates, most of whom were innocent of any crime, are known as the "victims of Yalta."

During the Big Three conference at Yalta on the Black Sea

in February 1945, the Allies promised to return any Russians liberated during their advance across Western Europe. Many Russians had come west during the war. Some had come voluntarily, like the Cossacks, to join Hitler against the Soviets. But most had come as prisoners of war, slave laborers, and men forced to serve in the German army. Stalin not only considered them all traitors, but a menace to Soviet power. They'd seen the hated West, and that knowledge would have to be kept from the Russian people at all costs. They were doomed.

The Allies knew how Stalin felt about his "traitors," but still agreed to return them. That decision was part of the cruel arithmetic of war. There was no telling how long the war with Japan would last, and they wanted Soviet help once the war finished in Europe. They were willing to trade that help for Russian lives, saving the lives of Allied soldiers in the process. It seemed the right thing to do at the time. Today the Allied governments are ashamed of their predecessors' actions. They should be.

Soon after the German surrender, the roundups began and the trains started rolling east. The Cossacks led the way. They at least had fought alongside the enemy. But their women and children hadn't. It made no difference. The Yalta agreement had to be followed to the letter, and immediately. Throughout 1946 and 1947, some 30,000 Cossacks were forcibly handed over to Stalin.

The most terrible incident took place in May 1947 in the Drau Valley of Austria, where the British gathered an additional 20,000 Cossacks. None wanted to return to the U.S.S.R., for they knew what lay ahead. As the trains waited, British troops forced the Cossacks to the railroad station. Now this was routine work for NKVD troops, but not for the British. They were tough men, Scottish Highlanders who'd seen all there was to see of war in North Africa and Italy. But nothing had prepared them for this! This was beastly, inhuman, offensive to their sense of honor. Yet their military discipline held firm. An officer reported how "terrified and hysterical people threw themselves on their knees before the soldiers, begging to be bayoneted or shot to death as an alternative to loading." Another told of men breaking down completely: "One or two of the soldiers just couldn't take it. There were soldiers pushing people along with rifle-butts—not hammering them but just pushing them—with tears streaming down their faces. It was the only time I ever saw an Argyll and Sutherland Highlander in tears."

Yet this was just the beginning. Rather than face Stalin's "justice," Cossacks killed themselves by jumping off a bridge into the Drau River. Several took their children with them. An eyewitness described one incident:

> A young woman with two small children ran to the edge. She embraced the first child for a moment, then suddenly flung him into the abyss. The other child was clinging to the bottom of her skirt and shouting, "Mama, don't! Mama, I'm frightened!" "Don't be afraid, I'll be with you," the frantic woman answered. One jerk of her arms and the second child was flying into the rushing waters of the river Drau. Then she raised her arms to make the sign of the cross. "Lord, receive my sinful soul," she cried, and before her hand reached her left shoulder she leapt in after her children. In a moment she was swallowed by the raging whirlpool.

The others were returned to Soviet authority. Most of the men were shot on arrival. The women and children were sent to Siberia. From 1945 to 1947, sealed trains sped eastward across Europe. Destination: Siberia. But this new wave of gulag slaves was different from the purge victims, the workers and peasants, the "politicals" who had come before. They had been easily cowed by their NKVD guards. The newcomers, however, were soldiers who knew how to stick together and fight back. In 1948, Boris Mekhtiev, a former colonel in the Red Army, led a rebellion in the coal-mining camps of Vorkuta. Thousands of prisoners took their guards' weapons, broke out, and headed for the Urals, where they intended to become guerrillas. Red fighter planes caught them on the open tundra and slaughtered them with machine guns. More was to come. Revolts, one involving 55,000 prisoners, continued until the mid-1950s, when living conditions finally improved in the camps. Not one of the revolts succeeded. The ringleaders were shot and their followers forced to work in handcuffs.

Rebuilding the Soviet Union wasn't easy. As we've seen, much of the country lay in ruins. The homeless tramped the roads and jammed railroad stations trying to find a place, any place, to live. Thousands of Muscovites lived in cellars with air holes opening at street level. Food was scarce. Although collective farms in White Russia and the Ukraine were brought back at gunpoint, farmers hated them and worked as little as possible. Whereas an American farmer could feed more than twenty people, a collective farmer produced only enough to feed four.

For Stalin, coal, steel, and oil came ahead of people's needs. He wanted a repeat of the First Five-Year Plan; that is, reconstruction was to be at the people's expense. In 1946 he called for a threefold expansion of industry above prewar levels. The Soviet Union must produce fifty million tons of pig iron, sixty million tons of steel, five hundred million tons of coal, and sixty million tons of oil. Increased production, he explained, was needed "to be sure that our motherland will be insured against all contingencies." Translation: the people had to make more sacrifices. For encouragement, he fed them a steady diet of propaganda. The capitalists were at the gates. Unless the Russian people sacrificed to the fullest, they'd attack. Industrial production rose, and with it the production of weapons.

Reconstruction in the Soviet Union went hand in hand with forcing Communism upon the peoples of Eastern and Central Europe. Even as the war raged, Stalin thought ahead, beyond victory. Thousands of trustworthy foreign Communists, many of them former Comintern officials, were trained to lead their countries after the Germans were driven out. Stalin meant to use them as the cement to bind their countries permanently to the Soviet Union.

Once the Red Army arrived, the people of Poland, Rumania, Hungary, and Bulgaria learned about liberation Stalin-style. Backed by Soviet guns, the Moscow-trained Communists set up "people's democracies." The only thing they had in common with democracy was the name. All political groups except the Communist Party were abolished and their leaders arrested. Elections, when held, were a farce; voters cast ballots for only one slate of candidates chosen by the Communist Party. The only freedom of expression was to say and print what the Communist rulers dictated. The secret police, modeled on the NKVD, kept tabs on everyone, and God help you if you said a word against the government!

These countries were so tightly bound to the U.S.S.R. that Westerners called them "satellites." Like the moon revolving around the earth, they depended upon the giant to the east. Stalin made sure that they served Soviet interests above all. The Red Army set up bases on their soil, where they remain to this day. Their economies were tied to the U.S.S.R.'s, which sent them oil and manufactured goods in return for raw materials. There was no choice: they had to trade with the

U.S.S.R., and on its terms, or not at all. Clearly, Soviet power was growing, menacing the democracies of Western Europe.

Winston Churchill sounded the alarm in March, 1946, during a speech at Westminster College in Fulton, Missouri. As President Harry Truman looked on, Churchill said:

> From Stettin in the Baltic to Trieste in the Adriatic, an iron curtain has descended across the continent. Beyond that line lie all the capitals of the ancient states of Central and Eastern Europe . . . what I must call the Soviet sphere, and all are subject in one form or another, not only to Soviet influence but to a very high . . . measure of control from Moscow.

Since, he continued, Moscow respected military might, the United States and Great Britain should continue their wartime alliance. Most Americans agreed. Public opinion polls showed that eighty-three percent of the people favored Churchill's idea of an alliance against the Soviet Union. His Iron Curtain speech marked the beginning of the Cold War, hostility between East and West just short of military conflict.

In March 1947, President Truman announced the Truman Doctrine, committing the United States to helping other nations resist Communist takeover. Three months later, Secretary of State George C. Marshall unveiled the Marshall Plan. Marshall, a professional soldier most of his life, understood that force alone could not check the support of Communism. Communism found openings wherever people were poor, hungry, and without hope. Marshall, supported by the president, aimed at resisting Communism by rebuilding war-torn Europe. Eventually twenty-two nations accepted Marshall Plan aid, at a cost to the United States of $10.2 billion. It was a bargain. When the program ended in 1951, Western Europe was well on the road of recovery.

The Cold War threatened to become hot when Stalin decided to test Allied determination. After the war, Germany had been divided into American, British, French, and Soviet zones of occupation. Berlin, which lay in the Soviet zone, was in turn divided among the four powers. In the spring of 1948, Stalin closed all road and rail links to the German capital. His aim in this "Berlin blockade" was to force the Allies to abandon the city.

President Truman would not bow to Soviet pressure. A stubborn man given to salty language, he called Stalin an "old SOB" and began an airlift to supply Berlin. Every day hundreds of American and British transport planes brought the food, fuel, and medicines needed to keep the city alive. By winter's arrival, 4,500 tons of supplies were arriving each day; by the spring of 1949, it was 8,000 tons, as much as had come overland before the cutoff. Seeing he was beaten, and unwilling to risk war at this time, Stalin ended the blockade.

The Berlin blockade was a turning point in history. Realizing that Stalin's Russia was a threat to world peace, twelve democratic countries formed the North Atlantic Treaty Organization—NATO—in April 1949. This military alliance consisted of the United States, Great Britain, France, Italy, Canada, Belgium, the Netherlands, Portugal, Denmark, Norway, Iceland, and Luxembourg. Greece and Turkey joined NATO in 1952, and in 1955 the Federal Republic of Germany became a member.

Joining NATO was an important step for the United States. True to George Washington's policy of forming no entangling alliances, the nation had never made a treaty pledging itself to go to war alongside another country. That policy ended in 1949. Eventually the United States made military alliances with forty-seven countries and stationed troops at 675 overseas bases. Americans had no choice, they believed, for only their country was able to match Stalin's war machine. American power became all the more important after August 1949 when the Soviets exploded their first atom bomb.

The democracies, however, were not Stalin's only opponents. Opposition came from within the Communist camp itself, and it made him furious. When the Nazis occupied Yugoslavia in 1941, guerrillas took to the mountains to carry on the resistance. The largest guerrilla force was led by Josip Broz, known as Tito, a veteran Communist. With the Nazi defeat, Tito took over the government. But unlike Eastern Europe, where communism was stuffed down people's throats by foreigners, Tito's brand of communism was very popular. As he'd shown during the war, he stood above all for Yugoslav independence—independence even from Moscow.

Stalin had other ideas. He wanted to control Yugoslav industry and use its natural resources for the benefit of the Soviet Union. When Tito objected, Stalin became enraged. He stormed about his Kremlin office, cursing that "insolent dwarf" for daring to defy him. "I will shake my little finger," he shouted at Nikita Khrushchev, "and there will be no more Tito. He will fall."

Stalin ordered an economic boycott, hoping to ruin Yugoslavia and bring her to her knees. He encouraged Yugoslav Communists to overthrow Tito. He sent Tito crude letters threatening him with Trotsky's fate. He even sent teams of terrorists to assassinate him.

Nothing worked; if anything, Tito grew stronger as the Yugoslav people rallied to him. The Allies did their share, too, giving Yugoslavia economic aid and letting it be known that they wouldn't stand by if Stalin invaded. Tito, for his part, cleaned house with an iron broom. Yugoslav Communist Party officials friendly to Stalin were fired; some went to jail and a few to the firing squad. His secret police rounded up the assassination teams. After one such roundup, the old guerrilla fighter wrote Stalin a private letter. That letter was found in a secret drawer in Stalin's desk after his death. It must have come like a slap in the face. Tito asked "Comrade Stalin" to stop, please, sending terrorists to kill him. "If this does not stop, I will send one man to Moscow and there will be no need to send another." It stopped, along with Stalin's efforts to turn Yugoslavia into a satellite.

Stalin also failed with China. Ever since the 1920s, he'd wanted a Communist China, but one he could control. Barring that, he preferred a weakened China under the existing Nationalist government of General Chiang Kai-shek, a dictator with close ties to the gangsters of Shanghai, who gladly murdered thousands of Chinese, including Communists, to please their friend. Besides, the tsars had seized vast territories in northern China during the nineteenth century and Stalin feared that a strong China would demand them back.

In October 1949, the Communists under Mao Tse-tung took power after a quarter-century of civil war. Mao announced the birth of the People's Republic of China in language all could understand: "The Chinese people have stood up. Never again will the Chinese be an enslaved people." Mao had no intention of knuckling under to anyone.

Stalin and Mao met in Moscow a month later. It was dislike, perhaps hatred, at first sight. Mao needed aid to rebuild China, but Stalin never offered anything without demanding something in return. Mao, he said, might be "another Tito," and he didn't want to support a possible enemy. At last they agreed to a $300 million loan payable with interest over five years— chicken feed compared to the Marshall Plan. In return, Mao agreed to let the Soviets keep control of Port Arthur and the Chinese Eastern Railway. "It was like taking meat from the mouth of a tiger," Mao said later, but it was the best he could get from the Russians. Stalin was also dissatisfied. He didn't trust Mao and, it seems, hoped to strengthen the Soviet position in Asia by starting trouble between China and the United States. The issue would be Korea.

Korea, a Japanese possession since 1910, was occupied by the Soviets and Americans after Japan's surrender in August, 1945. Like Germany, it was divided into zones of occupation, in which each side formed its own government. The Korean Democratic People's Republic—North Korea—had Soviet backing, while the Americans supported the Republic of Korea— South Korea. All foreign troops were removed by 1949, leaving the two governments to argue about which represented the entire Korean people.

The dictator of North Korea was Kim Il-sung, still in power in the late eighties. Kim was the Korean Stalin. Like Stalin, he described himself grandly as a worker of "countless legendary miracles," a "matchless iron-willed commander who is ever-victorious," and "the tender-hearted father of the people." It is unclear exactly what happened first, but many scholars believe that Stalin and Kim together decided to unite Korea by force.

On June 25, 1950, Kim's Soviet-trained army, spearheaded by swarms of T-34 tanks, Katyushka rockets, and MIG jet fighters, invaded South Korea. The United Nations condemned the action and asked member nations to send troops to South Korea's aid. Sixteen nations answered the call, with the United States sending 500,000 men, more than all the others combined.

Under the command of General Douglas MacArthur, U.N. forces routed the invaders and hurled them back across the border. When Kim rejected MacArthur's surrender demand, he invaded North Korea, driving all the way to the Yalu River, its boundary with China. As MacArthur advanced northward,

Mao, fearing an invasion, sent one million "volunteers" into Korea; these "volunteers" were actually the best troops in the Chinese People's Liberation Army. After savage fighting, a truce was worked out and both sides dug in near the original border.

The Korean War killed 34,000 Americans, 250,000 Chinese, and a million Koreans. It achieved nothing for anyone, including the man in the Kremlin. Instead of weakening China, as he'd hoped, it forced Mao to turn China into a first-rate military power. China tested its first atom bomb in 1963—but by then Stalin wasn't around to see the results of his policy.

Stalin celebrated his seventieth birthday during Mao's stay in Moscow. Never had the Chinese seen a man worshiped as he was during that winter of 1949. Hundreds of giant statues were erected in his honor, not only in the U.S.S.R. but in the satellite countries as well. Factories worked overtime, producing millions of smaller statues in plaster and iron for private homes. His picture was everywhere, and there was talk of a new calendar based, not on Christ's date of birth, but on Stalin's. Cannon boomed in salute and a million people marched across Red Square chanting, "Glory to Comrade Stalin!" "Forward to new victories under the leadership of Great Stalin!" "Stalin is Peace!"

He was the most powerful ruler on earth, yet power brought neither happiness nor peace of mind. Far from it. Stalin felt his seventy years, felt his health and vitality ebbing away. His face had become puffy, his ankles swollen, and his left arm now seemed to hurt all the time. He developed heart trouble and high blood pressure, which made his usually pale face look flushed. Worst of all were the slips of memory. He'd be with someone he'd known for years when suddenly he'd go blank.

"You, there, what's your name?" he once growled at Marshal Nikolai Bulganin, a close aide.

"Bulganin," was the reply.

"Of course, Bulganin. That's what I was going to say."

Stalin became very upset when this sort of thing happened. He didn't want others to notice, and they politely said nothing. But they knew.

Stalin was terrified. The man who'd brought death to millions couldn't face his own end. To reassure himself, he'd note that Georgians have been known to live 150 years. Whether he believed he would live that long is another matter.

Stalin's amusements were not those of a responsible adult, but of a pampered child who knows others must go along with his whims. It was his custom to have dinner after ten o'clock, and, since he couldn't stand eating alone, he invited his henchmen. They paid a price for their meals, not in money, but in self-respect. Stalin liked jokes, provided they were at others' expense. He'd look on, puffing on his pipe, as a guest sat on a tomato or a cake that had been placed on his chair. He especially liked to get people drunk; no one dared refuse drinks offered by the Great Stalin. Each guest had an NKVD man assigned to clean him up when he vomited and to take him home.

During the meal, Stalin might put a record on the phonograph. He was the nation's chief music critic, although he couldn't read music or play a musical instrument. No matter. A copy of every record made in the Soviet Union was sent to his office for review. He'd listen to them and write "good," "so-so," "bad," or "rubbish" on the label. Among his favorites was one of a woman singing with a chorus of howling, barking dogs.

Dinner over, the guests might be invited to see a movie. By then it was two o'clock in the morning, and they had to be at their desks on time for a full day's work, but everyone smiled and accepted the invitation. And so, field marshals, NKVD chiefs, and Communist Party bosses marched off to Stalin's private theater.

Stalin liked films. He viewed every film made in the U.S.S.R., and no film could be released without his approval. He had a private collection of American films, especially cowboy films and those of the comedian Charlie Chaplin. Tarzan films were his favorites and he owned a complete set of them. Guests often sat through two or three full-length films, which didn't make for a clear head at the office the next day.

Stalin never resumed his family life after the war. He never remarried and seems not to have been close to any woman after his wife's suicide. He refused to meet five of his eight grandchildren, possibly because they were partly Jewish; Yakov's wife and Svetlana's first husband were Jews. Vasily, his surviving son, was a problem even for Stalin. People called him "The Prince" and gave him anything he wanted, because they dared not offend Stalin's son. An air force captain at twenty, he was a general at twenty-four, although he didn't deserve either rank. Senior officers, even generals, who got in his way lost their posts or went to jail. He drank too much and in time became an alcoholic. Although Stalin scolded him like a little boy in front of others, he never mended his ways. Vasily died in 1962 at the age of forty-one after a drinking bout with some cronies from Georgia.

As Stalin grew older, his suspicions deepened to the point of mental illness. Bitter against the world, oppressed by fear, he didn't feel safe anywhere or with anyone. His security arrangements, alway tight, became tighter than any world leader's; not even Hitler had taken such precautions.

His house had more locks, gates, guards, guard dogs, bars, and barricades for its size than a maximum security prison. To confuse assassins, he had a number of identically furnished bedrooms, and slept in a different one each night. Thinking the air in his house might be poisoned, he had it scientifically analyzed. Even though all his food was tested in a laboratory, he still made his guests sample each dish before trying it himself.

And still he was insecure. Deep down he felt that everyone around him was evil. Either they wanted something for themselves, were plotting to ruin his work, or were out to hurt him. Like a cornered rat, he struck out at those closest to him. His old butler, an NKVD officer, was arrested as a British spy. His personal doctor was arrested as an American spy and kept chained in a dungeon. Instead of seeking medical care, he doctored himself with quack remedies. Some of his self-treatments were dangerous, as when he took steam baths, which increased his blood pressure and the strain on his heart.

Everyone fell under suspicion. The wives of Foreign Minister Molotov and other high officials were arrested to insure their husbands' loyalty. Stalin's two sisters-in-law, whom he'd known as children before the Revolution, were arrested and kept in solitary confinement. Their "crime," it seems, was knowing too much about his early life. Nor was Svetlana herself above suspicion. Her father once called her "a parasite" and accused her of making "anti-Soviet statements." Svetlana, wisely, didn't argue or ask where his information came from. It was useless; once he'd made up his mind, nothing could convince him otherwise.

Stalin's distrust finally turned inward. One day in 1951, Nikita Khrushchev saw him standing alone. "I'm finished," Khrushchev heard him mutter to no one in particular. "I trust no one, not even myself."

Suspicion reinforced his fears, fears increased his hatred, and hatred sharpened his thirst for blood. Stalin remained a killer to the end.

During the first weeks of 1953, Stalin planned a massacre

unlike any seen in peacetime. The survivors of the purge of
the 1930s had served him faithfully for a generation. They'd
lied for him, betrayed comrades for him, done his dirty work
without argument or complaint. They'd grown comfortable in
office and confident—more confident than he liked. Surely
they looked ahead to a future without Stalin. And it was only
natural that they should see themselves in his place.

What if one, or all, decided to hurry nature along? What
if they were plotting against him? What if they weren't true
Communists after all? As always with Stalin, those "what ifs"
were not questions. They were facts. If people *might* be plotting, that was proof that somewhere they *were* plotting.

Once against Stalin decided to purge the Communist Party
and the Soviet government. He'd start at the top with people
like Molotov, Beria, Voroshilov, and Khrushchev. Then he'd
work his way downward, through the rank-and-file Party members. Finally he'd purge the Russian people as a whole—purge
them as never before.

He began by dropping hints about his closest henchmen.
Molotov, he said, might be a British spy; so might Voroshilov.
Others might be "agents of American imperialism." Beria's
loyalty, too, was questioned because he'd let "enemies of the
people" slip through his fingers. The NKVD chief broke into
a frightened sweat. He'd seen Stalin set up others for the kill
and knew that these "hints" were advance death notices. "He's
going to wipe us all out," Beria told a Party comrade.

As with the Kirov assassination, Stalin planned to use a
faked murder plot to trigger the wider purge. This time he
meant to kill two birds with one stone. Like Hitler, he had a
fierce hatred of Jews. Soon after the war he began quietly to
attack the Jewish community in the Soviet Union. Yiddish,
the language spoken by most East European Jews, was in effect
banned. Yiddish theatres and newspapers were closed and books

no longer printed in that language. The number of Jews admitted to universities was severely limited and Jewish professors dismissed. Thousands of Zionists, those favoring a Jewish homeland in Palestine, found their homeland in the gulag.

Stalin's next step was to frame several well-known Jews and have them confess, implicating Communist bigwigs in their "crimes." He'd then use their confessions to incriminate all Soviet Jews, who'd be deported to Siberia. There he'd finish Hitler's work of extermination. Where fire and poison gas had failed, cold and overwork would succeed. Then it would be the turn of the Jews' Communist "accomplices." It was a devilish plan, and it almost succeeded.

On January 13, 1953, *Pravda* reported the arrest of several prominent Moscow doctors. Among them were six Jews, specialists in the Kremlin hospital, where most of the Soviet leaders went for treatment. They were charged with murdering a number of officials during "treatment" and of planning to murder Stalin himself on orders of the American and British intelligence services.

Pravda's report of the "Doctors' Plot" was a bombshell. No sooner did it appear then Stalin acted to "protect" the country. Mass arrests swept the U.S.S.R. as NKVD men hunted down "traitors." NKVD agents spread rumors that Jewish terrorists were preparing to blow up Moscow.

The public panicked. Within days, reports were coming in from everywhere about hospital patients refusing to take their medicine, or even fighting with Jewish doctors trying to "poison" them. Jews were insulted on the streets while policemen looked the other way. Meetings were held throughout the country to denounce the "doctor-murderers." Jewish children were often beaten up at school. Former Nazis read about these outrages, noting that it was like the good old days under their Fuehrer.

The accused doctors were tortured to make them confess and implicate others. Stalin was in a foul mood and not about to take no for an answer. When they balked, he called the chief interrogator to his office. "If you do not obtain confessions," he hissed, "we shall see that you are shortened by a head." Stalin wanted the questioners' methods to be as simple as possible. "Beat, beat and, once again, beat," he commanded. All confessed.

Then, as suddenly as it began, the tyrant's plot against the Soviet people collapsed. Stalin no longer called the tune.

Sometime in the early hours of March 2, Stalin sat alone in his room. Standing up, he felt a stabbing pain in his head as a blood vessel burst in his brain. Guards found him hours later sprawled on the carpet. He'd lost the power of speech and the right side of his body was paralyzed. He was dying.

"My father died a difficult and terrible death," Svetlana recalled, adding, "God grants an easy death only to the just." The bleeding in his brain gradually affected the centers that control breathing. Slowly, day after day, hour after hour, he suffocated. His face darkened, his lips turned black, and his features became twisted in agony.

At the last moment, he opened his eyes. They were filled with terror and rage and hatred. He looked at the strange doctors gathered around him. Svetlana, hastily summoned to his side, tells us that Beria, Khrushchev, and other leaders were also there. Suddenly he lifted his left hand and pointed menacingly, as if he were bringing down a curse on the whole world. It was the last thing he ever did. At 9:50 P.M., Thursday, March 5, 1953, Joseph Stalin died.

People were shocked when the announcement came over Radio Moscow. "I thought of all the dead relatives I had lost in the war," said a woman. "I cried and cried and cried. . . . It did me good." In the schools, in many classrooms, teachers and students cried together. Their tears were genuine. Stalin had been Russia's only ruler for nearly thirty years; for many, he was the only ruler they'd ever known. Already Lenin and the heroes of the Revolution were more like legends than real people. But Stalin was different. Russians had been taught to worship him from childhood, had sung his praises thousands of times. He'd led them to victory in the greatest war in history. Losing him was like losing a father, and it hurt.

Some inmates of the gulag cried, too. For years they'd known more about Stalin—the *real* Stalin—than other Soviet citizens. His passing lifted a weight from their minds, at least for a short time. A Zionist, tears streaming down his cheeks, kept repeating: "God has saved the Jews." Deep in a mine shaft in Vorkua, a slave smiled and said, "I have been here for nineteen years and this is the first good news I have heard." In a neighboring mine shaft an old man dropped to his knees in a puddle of water, shouting: "God be praised! There is still someone who thinks of us unfortunates!"

Stalin's mummified body was placed alongside Lenin's in the tomb in Red Square. It wasn't to stay there long.

At a secret meeting of the Twentieth Congress of the Communist Party in February 1956, Nikita Khrushchev, now Russia's ruler, took the speaker's platform. Khrushchev, for years Stalin's willing henchman, attacked his master as a way of bolstering his own position. The audience listened in silence as Khrushchev recited a catalogue of Stalin's crimes. Stalin had abused his power and created a "cult of personality." Great Stalin was a myth. The real man, he said, had been petty, distrustful, and "sickly suspicious." He'd killed indiscriminately, the good with the bad. The victims of his purge were good Communists forced to confess to crimes that existed only in his imagination. Stalin alone was responsible for the "unexpected" attack by Germany in 1941. The Doctors' Plot was a hoax aimed at destroying more innocents.

During the months and years that followed, the Russian people were gradually informed about Khrushchev's charges. True, Khrushchev hadn't discussed his own part in Stalin's crimes. Nor did he reject the use of terror as a legitimate tool of power; Stalin's sin was using terror when it wasn't necessary. But he'd begun to tell the truth, and that was a step forward.

"De-Stalinization"—the discrediting of Stalin and his policies—moved slowly. In October 1961 his body was removed from the tomb in Red Square. The coffin was placed in a pit dug near the Kremlin wall and filled, not with earth, but with tons of cement. Over it was placed a stone slab with the inscription: "J. V. Stalin."

Stalin's reburial was the signal for removing the monuments erected in his honor. His portraits were taken from public buildings. His statues were melted down. Cities, towns, factories, streets, and parks were renamed. Stalingrad, symbol of his arrogance, became Volgagrad. Only in his native Georgia can one still find a Stalin Street or a Stalin Park.

Despite de-Stalinization, the Soviet Union remains very much as he shaped it. The secret police, now called the KGB, is still a law unto itself. Freedom of religion remains little more than a phrase in the constitution. People still vote for only one, Communist, list of candidates in elections. The gulag still exists, although it contains thousands instead of millions and inmates are no longer deliberately worked to death. Mental hospitals have replaced Stalin's torture chambers and execution cellars. Those who protest abuses of human rights in the U.S.S.R. can be locked up with the insane, given fever-causing drugs, and placed in wet wraps that cause agonizing pain as they dry. Jews who ask to leave the U.S.S.R. are almost

always refused; they become "Refuseniks." They face countless
forms of persecution.

But Stalin is gone, and that in itself is reason to hope that
the Russian people can look forward to a happier future. Yet
where there is no democracy, no *true* democracy, there is
always the danger of a new Stalin arising.

That fear haunts Russian people. It haunted Yevgeny Yev-
tushenko, one of Russia's finest poets:

> *Double, triple the guard*
> *around this tomb!*
> *So that Stalin may never*
> *get out, nor the past*
> *with Stalin!*

It is not enough to keep Stalin's body entombed in cement.
His spirit must be locked up forever.

SOME MORE BOOKS

The Russian Revolution, the Soviet dictatorship, and Stalin are difficult subjects; so far as I know, no book covers them adequately for young readers. The books listed below, although written for adults, tell fascinating stories and amply repay the time spent with them.

Alliluyeva, Svetlana. *Twenty Letters to a Friend*. New York: Harper & Row, 1967.

Bethell, Nicholas. *The Last Secret: The Delivery to Stalin of Over Two Million Russians by Britain and the United States*. New York: Basic Books, 1974.

Brown, Anthony Cave, and Charles B. MacDonald. *On a Field of Red: The Communist International and the Coming of World War II*. New York: Harper & Row, 1981.

Carell, Paul. *Hitler Moves East, 1941–1943*. Boston: Little, Brown & Co., 1970.

———. *Scorched Earth: The Russo-German War, 1943–1944*. Boston: Little, Brown & Co., 1970.

Carmichael, Joel. *Stalin's Masterpiece: The Show Trials and Purges of the Thirties*. London: Weidenfeld and Nicolson, 1976.

Chamberlin, William Henry. *The Russian Revolution, 1917–1921*. 2 vols., New York: Grosset & Dunlap, 1965.

Clark, Alan. *Barbarossa: The Russian-German Conflict, 1941–1945*. New York: Morrow, 1965.

Conquest, Robert. *The Great Terror: Stalin's Purge of the Thirties*. New York: Macmillan, 1968.

———. *The Harvest of Sorrow*. New York: Oxford University Press, 1986.

———. *Kolyma: The Arctic Death Camps*. New York: Viking, 1978.

———. *The Nation Killers: The Soviet Deportation of Nationalities*. New York: Macmillan, 1970.

Craig, William. *Enemy at the Gates: The Battle for Stalingrad*. New York: E. P. Dutton, 1973.

Crankshaw, Edward. *Khrushchev: A Career*. New York: Viking, 1966.

———. *The Shadow of the Winter Palace*. New York: Viking, 1976.

Curtiss, John S. *The Russian Church and the Soviet State*. Boston: Little, Brown & Co., 1953.

Dallin, David J., and Boris I. Nicolaevsky. *Forced Labor in Soviet Russia*. New Haven: Yale University Press, 1947.

Djilas, Milovan. *Conversations with Stalin*. New York: Harcourt, Brace & World, 1962.

Engle, Eloise, and Pannanen, Lauri. *The Winter War: The Russo-Finnish Conflict, 1939–1940*. New York: Charles Scribner, 1973.

Gross, Jan Tomasz, and Irena Grudzinska-Gross. *War Through Children's Eyes: The Soviet Occupation of Poland and the Deportations, 1939–1941*. Stanford, Calif.: Hoover Institution Press, 1980.

Heller, Mikhail, and Alexandr M. Nekrich. *Utopia in Power: The History of the Soviet Union from 1917 to the Present*. New York: Summit, 1986.

Hingley, Ronald. *Stalin: Man and Legend*. New York: McGraw Hill, 1974.

Hosking, Geoffrey. *The First Socialist Society: A History of the Soviet Union from Within*. Cambridge, Mass.: Harvard University Press, 1985.

Howe, Irving. *Leon Trotsky*. New York: Viking, 1978.

Jonge, Alex de. *Stalin and the Shaping of the Soviet Union*. New York: William Morrow, 1986.

Khrushchev, Nikita S. *The Crimes of the Stalin Era*. New York: The New Leader, 1962.

———. *Khrushchev Remembers*. Boston: Little, Brown & Co., 1970.

Leggett, George. *The Cheka: Lenin's Political Police*. New York: Oxford University Press, 1985.

Lincoln, W. Bruce. *In War's Shadow: The Russians Before the Great War*. New York: Dial, 1983.

Medvedev, Roy A. *Let History Judge: The Origins and Consequences of Stalinism.* New York: Knopf, 1971.

Payne, Robert. *The Life and Death of Lenin.* New York: Simon & Schuster, 1964.

——. *The Life and Death of Trotsky.* New York: McGraw Hill, 1974.

——. *The Rise and Fall of Stalin.* New York: Simon & Schuster, 1965.

Powell, David E. *Antireligious Propaganda in the Soviet Union: A Study of Mass Persuasion.* Cambridge, Mass.: MIT Press, 1975.

Salisbury, Harrison E. *Black Night, White Snow: Russia's Revolutions, 1905–1917.* Garden City: Doubleday, 1977.

——. *The 900 Days: The Siege of Leningrad.* New York: Harper & Row, 1969.

Smith, Edward Ellis. *The Okhrana.* Stanford, Calif.: Hoover Institution Press, 1967.

——. *The Young Stalin.* New York: Farrar, Straus & Giroux, 1967.

Solzhenitsyn, Aleksandr I. *The Gulag Archipelago, 1918–1956.* New York: Harper & Row, 1973. Solzhenitsyn, a famous Soviet novelist, spent many years as a gulag prisoner.

Sublinsky, Walter. *The Road to Bloody Sunday.* Princeton, N.J.: Princeton University Press, 1976.

Tolstoy, Nikolai. *The Secret Betrayal, 1944–1947.* New York: Scribners, 1977.

——. *Stalin's Secret War.* New York: Holt, Rinehart & Winston, 1981.

Trotsky, Leon. *My Life.* New York: Pathfinder Press, 1970.

Tucker, Robert C. *Stalin as Revolutionary, 1879–1929.* New York: W. W. Norton, 1973.

Urban, G. R., ed. *Stalinism: Its Impact on Russia and the World.* Cambridge, Mass.: Harvard University Press, 1986.

Werth, Alexander. *Russia at War, 1941–1945*. New York: E. P. Dutton, 1964.

Wistritch, Robert. *Trotsky: The Fate of a Revolutionary*. New York: Stein & Day, 1979.

Zawodny, J. K. *Death in the Forest: The Story of the Katyn Forest Massacre*. Notre Dame, Ind.: University of Notre Dame Press, 1962.

INDEX